Winning the Study Game

Guide for Resource Specialists

A Systematic Program for Teaching
Middle School and High School Special Education Students
Study, Strategic-Thinking, Time-Management, and
Problem-Solving Skills.

Lawrence J. Greene

Peytral Publications, Inc.
Minnetonka, MN   55345
952-949-8707

Winning the Study Game – Guide for Resource Specialists   A Systematic Program for Teaching Middle School and High School Special Education Students Study, Strategic-Thinking, Time-Management, and Problem-Solving Skills.
                                                                By Lawrence J. Greene

Publisher's Cataloging-in-Publication
(Provided by Quality Books, Inc.)

Greene, Lawrence J.
  Winning the study game : guide for resource
specialists : a systematic program for teaching middle
school and high school special education students study,
strategic-thinking, time-management and problem-solving
skills / Lawrence J. Greene. – 1st ed.
  p. cm.
  ISBN: 1-890455-46-6

  1. Learning disabled teenagers--Education (Secondary)
2. Study skills--Handbooks, manuals, etc. 3. Special
education--Handbooks, manuals, etc. 4. Teaching--Aids
and devices.   I. Title.

  LC4704.74.G74 2002   371.9'0430281
                              QBI02-200427

Library of Congress Control Number: 2002107589
ISBN: 1-890455-46-6

Published by: *Peytral Publications, Inc.*
                 PO Box 1162
                 Minnetonka, MN   55345
                 (952) 949-8707
                 www.peytral.com

About the Author

After completing his studies in the Graduate School of Education at Stanford University, Lawrence J. Greene founded the Developmental Learning Center in Los Gatos, California. During the course of a career that spanned thirty years, he and his staff provided learning assistance to more than 14,000 underachieving students.

The author of thirteen books in the field of education, Lawrence Greene has also been an educational diagnostician, educational therapist, curriculum developer, university instructor, and consultant to school districts throughout the United States and Canada. In addition to the *Winning the Study Game Program*, Lawrence Greene's latest book *Roadblocks to Learning* was recently published by Warner Books. His new college study skills/life skills program will be published by Prentice Hall in the fall of 2003. Lawrence Greene can be contacted through the Peytral Publications, Inc. web page at www.peytral.com

Books by Lawrence J. Greene

Kids Who Hate School

Learning Disabilities and Your Child

Kids Who Underachieve

Getting Smarter

Think Smart, Study Smart

Smarter Kids

Improving You Child's Schoolwork

The Life-Smart Kid

Finding Help When Your Child is Struggling in School

Teachers' Desk Reference Guide to Learning Problems

Roadblocks to Learning

Winning the Study Game

Study Wise (2003)

Book Review Excerpts

Kids Who Hate School - *"None of the books I've read this season carries even a trace of the compassion and love of learning evidenced by learning disabilities specialist Lawrence J. Greene...Overall, the effect of this book on people concerned about learning disabilities will be one of enormous relief."* <u>San Francisco Chronicle</u>

Improving Your Child's Schoolwork - *"On most every topic, he has specific advice... His five pages on spelling problems is a model of diagnostic and prescriptive simplicity."* <u>Dallas Morning News</u>

Learning Disabilities and Your Child - *"Not only does Greene explain every possible issue related to learning disorders...he also presents a beautifully written and extremely moving series of case studies that will break your heart at the same time they fill you with relief."* <u>San Francisco Chronicle</u>

"An up-to-date and valuable resource for parents of the eight million children struggling with their school work because of learning dysfunctions." <u>Kirkus</u>

Getting Smarter - *"Practical lessons to help secondary students 'get smarter' ...Teachers will find these lessons appropriate for students at all ability levels."* <u>Curriculum Review</u>

"Each page is filled with solid and meaningful tips.... nicely done!" <u>Academic Therapy Newsline</u>

Kids Who Underachieve - *"Greene...has produced a treasure-trove of concrete, practical ideas for dealing with students who are underachieving for a variety of reasons... Parents and teachers will gain a wealth of information from this excellent book."* <u>Library Journal</u>

"This important book teaches us to diagnose learning problems early and take speedy action." <u>Los Angeles Times</u>

Smarter Kids - *"...[Greene] is masterful at explaining succinctly why some kids fail and some succeed."* <u>San Francisco Chronicle</u>

Table of Contents

Introduction

Most special education professionals who work with struggling students in grades one through six are preoccupied with teaching students the fundamentals. They have two primary goals: build an academic foundation that permits scholastically deficient students to learn more effectively and help students acquire the requisite skills to handle the mainstream curriculum. To achieve these objectives, special education professionals typically prioritize the basics: visual and auditory decoding, recall, comprehension, spelling, handwriting, math, and language arts.

Some students exit special education after a year or two of remedial assistance. Others with more intractable learning differences remain in resource programs or self-contained classrooms after transitioning into middle school. Although they may be mainstreamed in some or all of their classes, they continue to require learning assistance.

In most cases, remedial help at the middle school and high school levels is primarily tutorial and is designed to help students keep up with their classes. Resource specialists typically explain and reinforce content-area subject matter taught in mainstream classes and help students understand and complete in-class and homework assignments.

When the objectives of the special education program are attained, the safety nets are removed, and students are fully integrated into mainstream classes without further remedial support. Once students exit the special education program, they are essentially left to their own devices and are expected to fend for themselves.

The First Missing Piece: Effective Study Skills

Despite having made substantive academic gains, many students who discontinue special education programs are unprepared to meet the challenges that await them in mainstream classrooms. They may have mastered basic reading comprehension and writing skills, but they lack the higher level study and strategic-thinking skills that are requisite to their being able to work at a level commensurate with their full potential. These students haven't a clue about how to prepare for short-answer, multiple-choice, true/false, or essay tests. They do not know how to plan ahead, record assignments accurately, manage their time, or take notes from textbooks and class lectures. They do not set priorities or establish short- and long-term goals. They do not know how to identify what is important when they study and what is likely to be covered on a test. They don't know how to memorize key information. Lacking efficient study habits, these students are at a severe competitive disadvantage and are likely to struggle in middle school and high school, receive marginal grades, and become increasingly frustrated and demoralized.

The demands that fully re-integrated special education students face can be monumental. The daily battle to acquire new skills, handle course content, and complete difficult assignments can quickly exhaust their physical and intellectual energy. For many, effectual study and thinking skills are the icing on a cake that they may never get to taste.

Although some special education "graduates" continue to work diligently in their mainstreamed classes, others choose the path of least resistance and do the minimum possible. They do not complete their homework or submit their assignments on time. They do not check their work for careless mistakes. Many do not even bother to study at all, or, if they do study, they go through the motions mechanically.

<u>Symptoms of Deficient Study Skills</u>

Students do not:

- **record assignments accurately**
- **identify important information when they study.**
- **manage time efficiently**
- **plan ahead**
- **read with good comprehension**
- **memorize important information**
- **take effective notes from textbooks and lectures**
- **organize their materials**
- **meet deadlines**
- **proofread carefully and check for errors**
- **anticipate what's likely to be on tests**
- **write effectively**
- **develop a comprehensive test-preparation procedure**

The consequences of these deficits are predictable: poor motivation, ineffectual effort, marginal achievement, self-concept damage, lowered expectations and aspirations, and limited educational and career options.

Underachieving and non-achieving students may express their frustration and discouragement by turning off, acting out, becoming resistant, or retreating into their daydreams until the bell finally rings at 3:00 PM. That these youngsters often gravitate to others who are also doing poorly should come as no surprise. The sub-culture provides identity, reinforces shared maladaptive behaviors and attitudes, and offers the illusion of protection and security.

Each year hundreds of thousands of students exit special education programs and end up treading water in middle school and high school. Never having learned how to learn effectively, they equate studying with a mindless procedure of simply turning the pages in their textbooks.

The Second Missing Piece: Effective Thinking Skills

Students who learn passively and who have not been systematically taught how to think analytically, critically, and strategically stumble through school in a cerebral fog. Because they do not engage themselves in what they are learning, their capacity to comprehend, assimilate, retain, and utilize academic content is, at best, marginal. These students are unlikely to weigh the pluses and minuses of their options, make astute judgments, and apply cause-and-effect principles at critical decision points in life. As a consequence, they are at risk for acting thoughtlessly and impulsively not only in school, but also in the world outside of school.

<u>Symptoms of Deficient Strategic-Thinking Skills</u>

Students do not:

- **consider the potential consequences of their actions**
- **weigh the pluses and minuses of options and make wise choices**
- **handle challenges**
- **define concrete personal goals**
- **establish priorities**
- **create a practical strategy for getting from point A to point B**
- **focus their efforts or use their study time to maximum advantage**
- **analyze and solve problems**
- **learn from mistakes and bounce back from setbacks**

The Psychological Implications

Children who muddle through twelve years of school often bear deep emotional scars. Chronic frustration, unpleasant associations with test-taking, learning phobias, and diminished self-confidence are the common by-products of continually negative school experiences. Defeated learners characteristically devalue their talents, denigrate their intellectual potential, and lower their educational and career expectations and aspirations.

Even after learning problems have been ostensibly remediated, residual academic, study, and thinking-skills deficits can continue to erect barriers to scholastic achievement. Years of demoralization can leave an indelible psychological imprint, and the emotional overlay may continue to trigger self-defeating behaviors and attitudes long after students have been mainstreamed.

Most academically defeated students do everything in their power to avoid studying. Deluding themselves that they aren't really failing if they aren't really trying, they deny they have academic problems and simplistically contend that school is "dumb." Their rationalizations are, of course, transparent to astute teachers and parents.

Ironically, students with the greatest need to study diligently are usually the most resistant to doing so. They frequently procrastinate, act irresponsibly and thoughtlessly, and blame others for their difficulties. These behaviors, of course, accentuate the deficits they are attempting to hide, but self-sabotaging children are usually so psychologically enmeshed in their defense system that they fail to perceive this obvious paradox.

Smart Versus Intelligent

The commonly-held belief that intelligence is the primary determinant in school success discounts the vital role of focused effort and efficient study skills in the academic achievement equation. While it's true that the ability to grasp concepts, understand abstractions, perceive relationships, and recall information can facilitate learning and enhance school performance, it's also true that a superior IQ does not guarantee superior academic achievement. Brilliant children may perform marginally in school while their less-than-brilliant classmates may excel.

Students who have never struggled with learning problems have a much better chance of figuring out on their own how to succeed in school. Whether they acquire these insights intuitively, through osmosis, or by consciously or unconsciously modeling their behavior and attitudes on those of their parents, siblings, or peers is open to debate.

Unfortunately, the vast majority of LD students are unlikely to acquire these vital academic achievement skills naturally. These students must be methodically taught *how* to study and think more effectively. Guidance and practice are essential components in the instructional equation.

Students who are able to win in school join an elite club whose members are on a track that leads to good universities, rewarding careers, and a wide range of vocational options. They are motivated, diligent, and goal-directed, and their academic achievements significantly increase the likelihood that they will develop a positive self-concept. Tragically, far too many potentially capable special education "graduates" never make it into this exclusive achievers club because their school has failed to provide them with the full range of resources they need to succeed in school.

A Proven Intervention

As a special education professional, you realize that your students must one day compete in a world that can be harsh and unforgiving of those who lack motivation, skills, and self-confidence. You also realize that if your students are unable to function productively, they could easily end up at the bottom of the food chain.

Winning the Study Game provides you with an instructional program specifically designed to prepare special education students in grades six through eleven for successful reintegration into mainstream classes. The program systematically provides students with the study and thinking skills requisite to success in academically demanding mainstream middle school and high school classes. The methods have been carefully engineered to enhance learning efficiency, self-confidence, judgment, planning, problem-solving, time-management, and analytical, critical, and strategic-thinking skills.

The methods in the **Winning the Study Game Program** have been comprehensively field-tested for more than ten years with thousands of students. The program has unequivocally demonstrated that it can provide students with the essential tools they need to handle the regular curriculum and achieve academically.

<u>Basic Premises of the Winning the Study Game Program</u>

With systematic instruction, students who learn differently can be taught how to:

- **think strategically, analytically, and critically**
- **study productively**
- **learn efficiently**
- **apply cause-and-effect principles**
- **set goals**
- **establish priorities**
- **become organized**
- **manage time**
- **plan ahead**
- **solve problems**
- **think logically and rationally**
- **focus efforts**
- **learn actively and efficiently**
- **work conscientiously and diligently**
- **achieve academically**

<u>Description of Content</u>

The **Winning the Study Game Program** provides a step-by-step methodology for transforming passive learners into active learners. The workbook is divided into three sections. The first section, which consists of Units 1 - 5, focuses on creating an organized, time-efficient study system and a conducive environment for effective learning. The second section, Units 6 - 9, develops specific cognitive skills that are requisite to productive studying and effective test preparation. Students learn how to speed-read, improve their reading comprehension, take effective notes, identify important information, understand concepts, recall facts, anticipate what is likely to be on tests, and write powerful, well-organized essays that clearly express and encapsulate key information. The third section, Units 10 - 16, addresses issues related to problem solving, cause and effect, setting goals, establishing priorities, and strategic thinking.

Consisting of more than one hundred focused exercises and activities, the program teaches special education students how to think, study, and learn more productively. The exercises focus on teaching practical skills that have immediate application in the real world of the classroom and encourage students to become more aware and introspective. Repeated opportunities for practice, reinforcement, and mastery are integrated into the instructional strategy. Special education students are "set up" to succeed. Their successes generate self-confidence and stimulate effort and motivation. The goal is to empower students and convince them that they are capable of achieving in school.

Students can complete many of the activities independently or with minimal guidance. The program is designed to be resource specialist-student interactive, and the content is intended to be discussed. You are the guide and mentor in this process. Your role is to teach pragmatic, easy-to-learn and easy-to-apply achievement-oriented skills, stimulate analytical and strategic thinking, and nurture your students' intellectual development.

Teaching the entire Winning the Study Game Program requires approximately thirty hours of instruction. This instruction can be either one-on-one or small group. In only thirty hours, special education students can master effective, hands-on methods that can dramatically enhance their capacity to achieve in school and succeed in life.

The **Winning the Study Game Program** progresses systematically from basic to more advanced study and thinking skills. Students learn that handling homework is directly linked to planning, managing time, establishing priorities, and organization. They learn that good reading comprehension is linked to identifying important information and asking penetrating questions when they study. They learn that retention of key information is directly linked to capitalizing on their natural learning style and to effective note-taking. The skills are methodically presented and extensively reviewed, practiced, and reinforced.

Each unit incorporates high-interest anecdotes to which students can readily relate. The exercises are designed to be stimulating and thought-provoking, and this makes the process of mastering the fundamentals of efficient studying and thinking not only painless, but also fun.

As you know from personal experience, students do their best work when they're enjoying what they're learning, see the purpose for their effort, and are actively involved in the process. The **Winning the Study Game Program** incorporates these basic motivational principles. The book engages students and guides them to key insights about their current work ethic, study habits, attitudes, and performance. Insight alone, however, does not guarantee productive behaviors and attitudes. For meaningful attitude, behavioral, and performance changes to occur, students must be provided with repeated opportunities to practice, apply, and internalize the new skills that they are being taught.

The exercises and activities have been designed to produce repeated confidence-building successes. Your students will be able to see their own progress day-by-day. As their learning efficiency and thinking skills improve, their academic self-confidence and motivation will also improve. Your students will begin to see themselves as achievers, and they will realize that they are far more academically capable than they ever believed possible. Teenagers who are convinced that they can attain their personal goals are immediately distinguishable. They radiate self-assurance. They relish new challenges. They delight in their accomplishments. They want more. Success, they discover, is indeed addictive.

The Achievement Loop

Academic achievement is a continually recycling loop. Good skills and defined goals produce success. Success, in turn, produces self-confidence. Self-confidence stimulates motivation and effort and, in turn, produces more success. Stated differently, the more children accomplish, the more they believe in themselves, and the more they believe in themselves, the more they'll want to continue achieving. The feelings of pride and personal efficacy linked to achievement quickly become habit-forming. Successful students don't want to stop achieving because they like the associated feelings and want more. They are convinced not only that they *can* succeed, but that they *deserve* to succeed.

The opposite occurs when children are enmeshed in a non-achievement loop. This loop also continuously recycles itself. Poor skills and no goals produce little success. Little success produces diminished self-confidence, effort, and motivation, which, in turn, guarantee continued marginal performance. In other words, the more children fail, the less faith they have in themselves, and the less willing they are to stretch for the brass ring. Unfortunately, the negative experiences of students who have struggled for years with learning disorders usually cause them to become entangled in this non-achievement loop. The means for escaping from a non-achievement loop are self-evident: Students must be equipped with the essential study and thinking skills they need to win in school, and they must have repeated opportunities to experience success.

The Achievement Loop

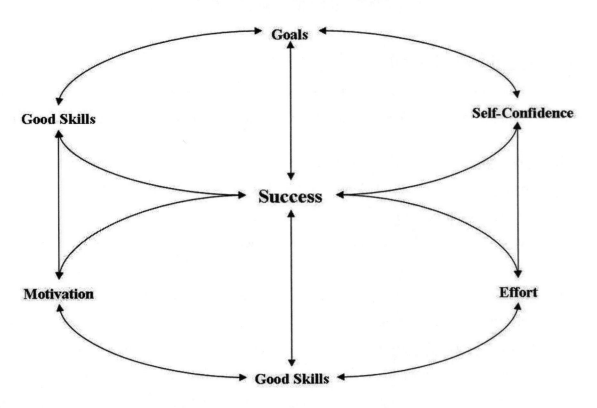

The Non-Achievement Loop

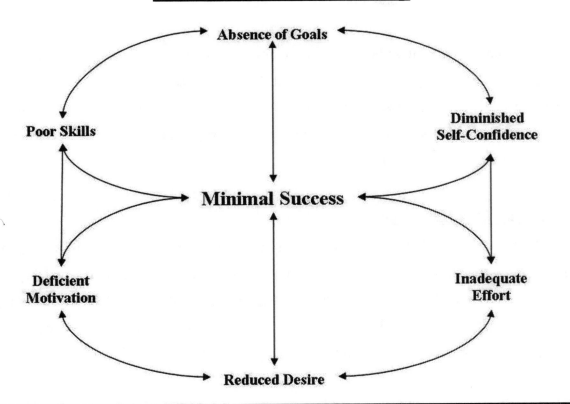

You will note that the arrows connecting the components point in two directions. This is intended to underscore how each element in the loop can affect each of the other elements.

The Instructional Method

The **Winning the Study Game Program** incorporates an instructional method called *cognitive behavior modification*. This teaching technique is based upon six teaching principles:

1. **Relevancy** -- The skills directly relate to the challenges students confront every day.

2. **Insight** -- The program demonstrates that the skills being taught can make school easier, more productive, and more rewarding.

3. **Instruction** -- The methods are presented in a systematic sequence to assure comprehension.

4. **Reinforcement** -- The program offers repeated opportunities to practice to assure mastery and assimilation.

5. **Behavior Modification** -- The methods develop productive behaviors through methodical practice and carefully orchestrated opportunities for success.

6. **Application** -- The program offers repeated opportunities to use the skills being taught in order to assure habituation.

The objective of cognitive behavior modification is to guide students to the realization that the skills they are learning are valuable and that the procedures can make their lives easier and more rewarding and productive. This paradigm shift from responding passively and feeling oppressed to responding receptively and being actively engaged in the learning process is vital to students becoming motivated and goal-focused.

How to Use This Resource

The Resource Specialist Guidelines present an overview of the objectives of each unit, examine the activities in the unit, suggest a basic lesson plan, and illuminate the key issues. Answer keys are provided when appropriate. Each anecdote and activity focuses on developing skills in a specific area. Although you may choose to read aloud certain sections, it is recommended for obvious reasons that your students do most of the reading.

This book is written at approximately the beginning-5th-grade reading level. Children with significant reading problems will obviously require extra assistance. On occasion you'll discover words highlighted by asterisks. These are marked because they may be unfamiliar or confusing to your students and should be discussed. Some exercises are optional and can be used for reinforcement of concepts and skills or for remedial purposes with students who are having difficulty mastering concepts and procedures.

The **Winning the Study Game Program** provides repeated opportunities for students to assimilate and master each skill being taught. The material encourages students to "stretch" intellectually. Although this stretching stimulates intellectual growth, it can also produce frustration and discouragement if students are asked to reach too far. For this reason you must obviously exercise judgment in determining the pacing of the instruction and the quantity of material being covered in each session.

Enough said.

<u>Important Notes</u>:

1. **At the end of the student introduction, students are instructed to insert the workbook into their binders. The workbook has been three-hole punched to facilitate this. Students should be encouraged to review and refer to appropriate sections in the book whenever they are confronted with a difficult assignment, a challenging exam, or a seemingly intractable problem. Encourage your students to keep the book and to place it in their binder at the beginning of each year throughout middle school and high school.**

2. **Important forms (e.g. My Weekly Schedule, My Personal Study Assignment Sheet, etc.) used in the Student Workbook can be found in the Appendix of this guide. These forms may be photocopied. Permission to duplicate appears at the bottom of the form.**

Part 1

Getting Organized

Teaching Notes

Unit 1: Developing a Personal Study Plan

Objectives:

This unit shows resource-program and special-day-class students how to create a study schedule that will allow them to manage and organize their time more efficiently. Students make realistic predictions about how much time they need each day to complete their assignments, and they use this data to create an appropriate study strategy.

Basic Lesson Plan

Student Book pages 4-20

Appendix page 108 - My Weekly Schedule
page 109 - My Study Schedule Contract

1. Students read the introductory anecdote--**THE DAILY HOMEWORK BATTLE.** They list and evaluate each maladaptive behavior and attitude that is described and make predictions about the consequences of the student's *modus operandi*.

2. In the section entitled **THINKING AND PLANNING AHEAD,** students estimate their weekly study requirements in each subject and compute their required daily study time. Guidance will be required during this estimation activity, especially in the case of students whose analytical thinking and critical judgment are off-base.

3. Students follow a *nine-step procedure* for creating an effective personal study schedule. Using the "Sample Study Schedule" as a model, they then create their own "Weekly Study Schedule."

4. Students read and sign a "Personal Study Schedule Contract" that commits them to a minimum two-week trial of their schedule before they make adjustments.

5. Students examine the issue of reasonable versus unreasonable study breaks when doing homework. A general "study break formula" is suggested. For some students this formula is realistic. For others with significant learning deficiencies and concentration deficits, the formula can serve as a goal. Students then complete a true/false exercise that encourages them to review and consider what they have learned about planning, scheduling, and time-management.

The Residual Effects of Learning Problems

The emotional, behavioral, and academic implications of learning problems are self-evident. Learning disorders are a primary source of marginal academic performance, inefficient thinking, and counterproductive behavior. Students who struggle to read accurately, comprehend the content of their textbooks, express their ideas verbally and in writing, solve math problems, recall information, and follow instructions are clearly at a profound competitive disadvantage. This disadvantage may persist even after their underlying perceptual processing deficits have been ostensibly remediated.

Emotionally and academically vulnerable children will do whatever they can to protect themselves from feeling worthless and incompetent. Many will attempt to hide their learning deficiencies by procrastinating and acting irresponsibly. These youngsters usually present as being unmotivated and resistant. For many discouraged learners, the unconscious mindset is "if I don't really try, I can't really fail."

Parents and classroom teachers who have a marginal understanding of the implications of learning disabilities may conclude that the self-defeating conduct is the *source* of the struggling child's academic problems. This conclusion is flawed. Most counterproductive behaviors and attitudes are *symptoms* of imprinted negative associations with learning. Even extreme and seemingly willful irresponsibility usually reflects an unconscious defensive response to persistent feelings of inadequacy, hopelessness, and despair.

Students who are enmeshed in a daily battle to survive scholastically rarely possess the objectivity to recognize that their self-protecting conduct actually calls attention to the deficiencies they're attempting to hide. Their instinct is to protect themselves, and from the vantage point of academically defeated students, procrastination, irresponsibility, and lack of motivation may appear to be their only recourse. The primary concern of many of these children is "how do I get through today without letting everyone see how dumb I am?"

The consequences of struggling students entrapping themselves in an elaborate system of defense mechanisms and compensatory behavior can be life-altering. Defended children who are convinced that they cannot succeed are at risk for shutting down in school. Acquiescing to marginal achievement, they simply lower their educational and vocational expectations and aspirations and then retreat into a psychologically protective comfort zone.

The antidote is to provide students who learn differently with the essential study habits and learning skills they need to prevail scholastically. To master and internalize these academic survival skills, students require focused, systematic instruction, on-going feedback, and repeated opportunities to practice.

Self-Discipline

To handle the mainstream academic curriculum successfully, students in special education programs must be taught how to manage their time efficiently, meet deadlines, and complete their work. Those who do not acquire these self-regulation and planning skills are destined struggle in their mainstream classes.

Behaviors and Attitudes That Signal Planning Deficits:

- **Procrastination**
- **Difficulty establishing short- and long-term goals**
- **Difficulty establishing priorities**
- **Inadequate time management**
- **Inadequate preparation**
- **Incomplete assignments**
- **Late assignments**
- **Chronic disorganization**
- **Inattention to details**
- **Irresponsibility**
- **Flawed judgment**
- **Repeated miscalculations**

In some instances, chronic planning deficits may be attributable to ADD/ADHD. In other instances, students may be unfocused and disorganized because they have failed to internalize a basic cause-and-effect principle: *Success in any demanding endeavor requires careful planning, preparation, and execution.* Academically deficient students rarely perceive the obvious link between their late, sloppy, incomplete, or inaccurate assignments and the poor grades that result from their careless and cavalier attitudes about their obligations and responsibilities.

Chronically irresponsible students can be masterful at defending and rationalizing their counterproductive behavior. The classic excuses typically include:

- **"The work is boring or stupid."**
- **"I am trying! But my teacher is unfair."**
- **"I forgot...."**
- **"My teacher didn't tell us it was due today."**
- **"My teacher didn't explain this."**
- **"Don't worry. I'll get it done."**
- **"My teacher said that doing it this way was OK."**
- **"My teacher didn't assign any homework today."**

These rationalizations and evasions allow marginally performing students to avoid taking responsibility for their maladaptive attitudes and behaviors. By blaming and making excuses, they attempt to convince themselves and others that everything is OK. This illusion invariably shatters when report cards are sent home.

With systematic instruction and sufficient practice, most special education students can acquire more productive time-management skills. They can be taught how to plan ahead and budget their time more efficiently. This is the critically important first step in preparing them for successful integration into academically demanding mainstream classes.

Activities and Exercises

The Daily Homework Battle

Student Book page 4

This exercise underscores how time management and organization are linked by fundamental cause-and-effect principles. The anecdote describes a child who is clearly having difficulty managing his time and responsibilities. Students critically analyze and assess Joshua's maladaptive behavior and make predictions about what is likely to happen. This evaluative procedure, which is used throughout the program, is designed to encourage them to think critically about their own behavior.

Thinking and Planning Ahead

Student Book page 9

In this exercise, students learn the procedures for developing an efficient study plan. The activity introduces the "nuts and bolts" of productive time-management. Students are guided to a key insight: They can make their lives easier by planning ahead.

The first step in designing a personal schedule is for students to estimate the amount of daily study time in each subject that Joshua, the student described in the introductory anecdote, should spend to do a first-rate job. Students estimate the weekly time required to get a good grade on a Friday vocabulary quiz and then divide this time by four (Monday through Thursday) to determine the average daily study time that's required. You will obviously want to examine carefully this time-averaging procedure with your students. For practice, you might have them use the same procedure to determine the average study time they need to spend each evening in at least one other subject area before having them do the remaining math computations on their own. Students with significant learning differences are likely to require more assistance and supervision. The questions at the end of the exercise are designed to reinforce the cause-and-effect link between the efficient use of time, careful planning, and improved school performance. This linkage is repeatedly underscored throughout the program.

Making Your Own Study Schedule

Student Book page 12

Students are now ready to create a personal study schedule. In this exercise, they apply the planning procedures they have learned in analyzing their own personal study requirements, and they practice a nine-step procedure for creating a schedule tailored to their personal needs. They estimate the average amount of time they must study every evening in each subject and transfer these projected time requirements to a daily study schedule. The steps are clearly enumerated, but students may require additional explanations and demonstrations. It is recommended that you photocopy extra practice copies of the "Study Schedule," in case the students make mistakes in coloring and coding their schedules. (See Appendix for materials.)

My Personal Study-Schedule Contract

Student Book page 18

After having developed a reasonable and practical study schedule, students are asked to sign a "contract." This contract, which commits them to utilize the schedule for two weeks before making adjustments, encourages on-going use of the schedule until the time-management habits are imprinted. After two weeks of experimentation, students fine-tune their schedule and use this revised schedule for four weeks before making further revisions.

The objective of this unit is to help students discover that schedules are not an adult conspiracy designed to make their lives miserable. Ideally, students will realize that using a schedule does not have to be painful, boring, restrictive, or unfair.

Study Breaks

Student Book page 18

The frequency and duration of study breaks are issues that should be examined and discussed. Your students' attitudes may be radically different from your own, and you should encourage them to share their views in a non-judgmental context. Students who must continually struggle to learn and those who have ADD/ADHD are likely to have very painful associations with homework and studying. These students are also likely to do everything possible to avoid the associated pain. This would include chronic procrastination and taking excessive study breaks.

Ideally, your students will come to the realization that they must exert self-discipline if they are to study productively. You might want to suggest the described study break formula, assuming, of course, that you concur with it. If you don't, feel free to modify the formula. Urge your students to integrate the formula into their personal study plan. They might experiment with the formula to see if it works for them. The final exercise--**WHAT I HAVE LEARNED ABOUT SCHEDULES**--encourages students to think analytically, critically, and strategically about the issues and procedures that were introduced in the unit.

Teaching Notes

Unit 2:   Recording Your Assignments

Objectives:

This unit provides students with a practical system for recording their assignments. It also provides opportunities for them to practice and refine their homework-recording skills.

Basic Lesson Plan

Student Book pages 21 – 34

Appendix page 110 - Practice Assignment Sheet
         page 111 - My Personal Assignment Sheet

1.   Students read **KNOWING WHAT YOU'RE SUPPOSED TO DO AND WHEN IT'S DUE.**

2.   In **PREDICTING WHAT WILL HAPPEN,** students underline and number each of Maria's behaviors as the teacher is giving a homework assignment. They write down each behavior, evaluate it, and make predictions about the consequences of the behavior.

3.   Students underline each of Heather's behaviors as the teacher is writing down the homework assignment. They write down each behavior, evaluate it, and make predictions about the consequences of the behavior.

4.   In **CREATING A PERSONAL HOMEWORK-RECORDING SYSTEM,** students brainstorm ideas for helping Heather improve her grades.

5.   Students examine the *Sample Assignment Sheet* and using it as a model, they transfer a facsimile assignment to the *Practice Assignment Sheet*.

6.   In **MASTERY: MORE PRACTICE WRITING DOWN ASSIGNMENTS,** students record a more extensive assignment. They examine and then use a list of common abbreviations that can save them time and space when they record their assignments on their assignment sheet. They then take a quick review quiz to reinforce what they've learned about recording assignments effectively.

Confusion and Chaos

Students who have learning problems often haven't a clue about what their teachers expect from them. This does not mean that they haven't been explicitly told what their assignments are and when their work is due.

The homework assignment confusion can usually be attributed to four factors:

- **Students are struggling with perceptual processing deficits that undermine their ability to record their homework accurately and completely.**

- **Students are afflicted with ADD/ADHD, and this condition interferes with their ability to stay focused and attend to details.**

- **Students have never been methodically taught how to record their assignments properly.**

- **Students are refusing to use the homework recording system they've been taught.**

Students who learn differently and who have poor study habits often share maladaptive traits that significantly increase the likelihood of their performing marginally in school. They typically:

1. **do not follow instructions**
2. **submit incomplete work**
3. **"forget" to do assignments and study for tests**
4. **fail to meet deadlines**

Whereas achieving students can often figure out with little or no formal instruction how to create an effective homework-recording method, most students in resource programs lack this intuitive capacity. These students must be methodically taught how to record their assignments accurately and efficiently, and they must be provided with repeated opportunities to practice. This repetition and reinforcement are essential if their behavior is to be productively modified.

Some students who learn differently may appear quite cavalier about not paying attention to the important details that can determine whether they receive a good or a poor grade. Without intervention and cognitive behavior modification, their nonchalant attitude and carelessness could become entrenched habits that are likely to have dire long-range academic and vocational consequences.

An English teacher may write the following homework assignment on the chalkboard.

English Assignment

Exercises at the end of Unit 1, Chapter 2. Do odd numbered questions (#'s 1, 3, 5, 7 and 9). Complete sentences. Skip line between each answer. Put name on the upper right-hand line and date below it. Due tomorrow.

Students who believe that they can remember the information may not record the assignment or may simply write: "Unit 1, Chapter 2. Do exercises." Having omitted vital information and instructions, these students will probably submit work that does not conform to the clearly stated directions

To make certain that your students record assignments properly in their mainstream classes, you will need to provide them with clear and easy-to-follow guidelines. You will also need to supply encouragement, affirmation for progress, supervision, feedback, and extensive opportunities for practice. Once students master the system and experience the payoffs, most will use it voluntarily.

Activities and Exercises

Predicting What Will Happen

Student Book page 22

The introductory anecdote examines and contrasts two very different students. Students indicate and evaluate each girl's attitudes and behavior and predict the consequences.

The goal of the exercise is to encourage students to evaluate their own assignment-recording skills and to stimulate critical thinking about their *modus operandi*. Students must be guided to the realization that they can choose to function in ways that improve the likelihood of their achieving in school or in ways that diminish their chances.

Creating a Personal Homework-Recording System

Student Book page 24

In this exercise, your students brainstorm specific ideas that might help Heather improve her performance in school. As you discuss the options with your students, emphasize that certain procedures, such as methodically recording assignments, ensure that students will have the information they need to complete their homework properly.

There are, of course, several different systems for recording homework assignments. The system presented in this book and the design of the assignment sheet (see Appendix) represents one particular format. If you prefer a different one, you should certainly feel free to substitute it.

Providing a precise model for recording assignments is vital. Initially, students who learn differently will need to be closely monitored to make certain they're following the procedures correctly. Once they demonstrate that they have mastered the homework-recording system, they can modify and individualize the procedure.

Practice Writing Down Assignments
Student Book page 25
Mastery: More Practice Writing Down Assignments
Student Book page 28

These exercises provide opportunities for additional hands-on practice. Students are asked to record a facsimile of an entire week's assignments in a Practice Assignment Sheet. As they proceed through the steps, they will require supervision and feedback. If they choose to use abbreviations, shorthand, or a personal code, emphasize that they must be able to decipher and understand what they write and that they must include the vital information.

With sufficient practice and guidance, your students will become increasingly adept at recording their assignments efficiently. In time, the procedure of systematically writing down key information will ideally become second nature.

Completing Your Personal Assignment Sheet
Student Book page 31

The final step is for students to make the transition from practice to actual utilization of the assignment-recording techniques in their mainstream classes. Periodic supervision to make certain that they are using the methods is vital, especially in the case of students who have a tendency to be chronically inattentive and disorganized.

The unit ends with a review activity entitled **What I Have Learned about Recording Assignments**. This exercise is designed to reinforce the methods that have been taught.

Students who acquire effective self-management skills and self-discipline and who attend to details have a distinct advantage over those who function mindlessly and haphazardly. Good homework-recording skills are vital to school success and can have an immediate, direct, and positive impact on the quality of your students' schoolwork. Poor homework-recording skills, on the other hand, can exacerbate the effects of learning problems, cause grades to be lower, and result in perennial underachievement.

Once students have mastered the assignment-recording system, encourage them to continue using the system. The goal is obviously for recording assignments to become an entrenched habit.

Copies of the assignment sheet should be handed out, and students should be required to use the system to record their actual weekly assignments on their assignment sheet. This should be presented as an experiment that will last for a week. The merits of the system should then be discussed. Require students to continue using the homework recording system after making minor modifications and personalized fine-tuning. As you examine each student's assignment sheet, you should provide guidance, feedback, acknowledgment, and affirmation.

Continued monitoring will ensure that your students are using the system effectively and consistently in the weeks and months ahead. If your school has its own standardized system for recording assignments that all students are required to use or if you already have taught your students how to record assignments, you can, of course, bypass this unit.

<u>Teaching Notes</u>

Unit 3: Organizing Your Study Materials

Objectives:

This unit underscores the importance of organization and having access to the materials needed to do homework efficiently. It provides students with practical step-by-step methods for creating more order in their lives and enhancing their efficiency when they study.

<u>Basic Lesson Plan</u>

Student Book pages 35-45

Appendix page 112 - Checklist #1 - Materials to Bring Home
          page 112 - Checklist #2 - Materials to Bring to School
          page 113 - Checklist #3 - Home Study Environment

1. Students read **HAVING THE TOOLS TO DO THE JOB.** They examine Justin's study behaviors, identify his specific actions, evaluate his homework procedures, and predict the possible or probable consequences of his homework *modus operandi*.

2. In **MAKING CERTAIN YOU HAVE THE NECESSARY MATERIAL**, students determine the material they need to do their homework and study effectively. They then practice applying organizational principles by using three checklists during a one-week experiment.

3. Students organize their binders and label sections in their notebooks. They place copies of their study schedules and organizational checklists in the front of their binders.

<u>Organization and Productivity</u>

Academic achievement and good organizational skills are intrinsically linked. Successful students plan ahead. They develop a system for recording their assignments, and they consistently use the system. They also have, if not a formal study schedule, at least a mental study schedule that indicates approximately how much time they need to spend each evening doing homework. At the end of the school day, good students make sure they take home their assignment sheet, textbooks, and binder. When they sit down to do their homework, they make sure they have access to a pen, pencil, paper, ruler, and dictionary.

Students who learn differently, and especially those with ADD/ADHD, are often at the other end of the organization and efficiency spectrum. They are likely to forget to bring home their textbooks and important papers. Their desks are a mess. Their rooms are a disaster area. Their binders are in disarray. If they have an assignment sheet, it is usually incomplete, inaccurate, and illegible.

Students whose lives are cluttered and disordered typically spend more time looking for things than they do completing their work. The consequences are predictable: marginal work and stress for everyone affected by their behavior.

Lecturing about the value of organization to struggling, chronically disorganized students is generally a waste of time. Those with the greatest need to change counterproductive behaviors are usually most resistant to change. Associating advice with nagging, they are likely to tune out and insist on doing it their way.

Patterns of disorganization established in childhood frequently become hard-to-break habits that persist throughout life. To break these counterproductive habits, resource specialists must:

1. **Provide clear organizational guidelines**
2. **Show students how to use study materials efficiently**
3. **Provide opportunities for practice organizational procedures**
4. **Demonstrate that improved organization can save time and improve grades**
5. **Acknowledge and affirm progress**

Chronically disorganized students who study surrounded by chaos must be guided to the realization that order and enhanced organization can make their lives easier and provide desirable payoffs. The starting point in the process of reorienting their counterproductive behavior is to provide them with a practical and accessible model for becoming better organized and to teach them specific, hands-on techniques for organizing their notebooks and managing their at-home study area.

With systematic instruction, sufficient practice, carefully orchestrated successes, and affirmation for improvement, disorganized students who learn differently will begin to see themselves as being capable of creating order in their life. Once this critically important shift in mind-set occurs, these students will see the practical organizational procedures as allies and not as some sinister plot designed by their teachers, resource specialists, and parents to make their lives miserable.

Changing behavior is like breaking in a new baseball glove. Kids need to pound it, oil it, and shape it. It takes time before the glove fits right and feels comfortable. Students who are disorganized will need to go through a similar pounding, oiling, and shaping procedure. They will need time to mold the new organizational behaviors until they "fit," feel comfortable, and are fully functional.

Students who experience first-hand the benefits of organization are far more likely to become converts than those who are assaulted with lectures or sermons. As they become better organized, these students will discover that they are studying more efficiently and effectively. The objectives are for them to appreciate the direct cause-and-effect link between order, productivity, and good grades and to modify their counterproductive behaviors.

Activities and Exercises

Examining Someone Else's Study Procedure

Student Book page 37

Identifying the Specifics

Student Book page 37

Evaluating Another Person's Study Style

Student Book page 40

Predicting What Will Happen

Student Book page 40

In these exercises, students examine an anecdote that describes a student with productive study behaviors. The student, however, procrastinates about doing his homework because he finds the work difficult. Nonetheless, once he begins to study, he gets the job done efficiently and effectively. Students identify his specific behaviors, evaluate his study procedures, and predict the consequences.

Making Certain You Have the Necessary Materials
Student Book page 41

Students examine three simple checklists and personalize the checklists by adding appropriate content based upon their own needs. These checklists indicate the materials they should bring home from school, take to school, and have available when studying. Students then experiment for a week using the checklists each day to make certain they've created a context at home conducive to efficient studying. During the experiment, they should keep track of their performance (i.e., grades on homework and tests). At the end of the experiment, encourage them to express their feelings about the system and its effect on their performance. With practice, the checking-off procedure will become a habit they can perform mentally without having to use a formal checklist. This "carrot" of not having to use the formal check-off system should reduce resistance and facilitate internalization of more efficient behaviors. Some chronically disorganized students, however, may need to use the actual checklists for a more protracted period until the positive behavioral changes are fully internalized and assimilated. Students with ADD/ADHD will need to be more closely monitored to make certain they are using the checklists everyday.

Organizing Your Binder
Student Book page 43

In this section, your students learn a step-by-step procedure for efficiently organizing their binders. Highly disorganized students will require more careful monitoring to make certain they are performing the steps properly and using the procedure consistently. Students then answer a series of true-false statement that review and reinforce the organizational principles that have been taught in the unit.

Answers to True/False Statements

1. F	3. T	5. F	7. F	9. T	11. F	13. F
2. F	4. T	6. F	8. F	10. F	12. F	14. F

Teaching Notes

Unit 4: Creating the Best Study Environment

Objectives:

This unit shows students how to create a studying context that supports efficient learning and guides them to the realization that such a context can help them improve their grades.

Basic Lesson Plan

Student Book pages 47-63

**Appendix page 114 - Keeping Track of My Performance During the Experiment
        page 115 - My Personal Performance Chart**

1. Students read **OPERATING BELOW PEAK PERFORMANCE** and then critically evaluate Kenesha's study habits, make predictions, examine different perspectives, and present ideas for improving the study environment.

2. In **DOING SEVERAL THINGS AT ONCE,** students examine hypothetical situations that require concentration and predict the consequences of diverting attention from the task at hand.

3. Students examine the positive payoffs derived from creating a quiet "study fortress."

4. In **WHAT'S RIGHT IN THIS PICTURE**, students describe in detail an illustration of a study environment in which distractions have been reduced.

5. In **WHAT'S WRONG IN THIS PICTURE,** students examine an illustration of a highly distracting study environment and identify specific conditions that could interfere with effective studying.

6. Students list the ways in which they might improve their own study environment at home.

7. Students implement their ideas for creating more order in their study environment and do an experiment in which they keep track of their performance on homework

assignments and tests. They examine a facsimile chart that plots test and homework grades and then plot their own grades on a chart. The final activity consists of a review exercise that reinforces the procedures that have been presented in the unit.

Reducing Distractions

Students rarely derive benefit from their studying when they continually allow themselves to become distracted. Attempting to write an essay, memorize vocabulary definitions, or do math problems while watching TV, listening to loud music, making telephone calls, and taking repeated trips to the kitchen is typically an exercise in futility. The consequences of being surrounded by distractions are especially acute in the case of ADD/ADHD students.

Ironically, students with the greatest need to concentrate are usually the most predisposed to surrounding themselves with distractions. These students are also likely to be the most vehement in arguing that they can study efficiently when their attention is diverted.

Some educators support these "environment doesn't matter" rationalizations and contend that children in modern American society have become so habituated and inured to sensory bombardment that they can actually work effectively under these less-than-ideal conditions. Most resource specialists, who deal everyday with the debilitating academic deficiencies of struggling learners, would vigorously debate this position and would argue that studying efficacy is demonstrably undermined when students study in a highly distracting context.

Students can be taught practical methods for managing their at-home study environment and intentionally eliminating or reducing the stimuli. These methods will not resolve the chronic distractibility associated with ADD/ADHD, but they can significantly benefit students who work ineffectually because they have simply not figured out the logical "do's and don'ts" of productive studying.

Lectures and sermons about the need for good study habits are generally ineffectual. The advice is rarely heeded, and the admonitions usually do little more than trigger defensiveness and active or passive resistance. The alternative is to guide students to the realization that they can significantly improve their school performance by intentionally limiting distractions. Students who discover that a few simple distraction-reducing steps can improve their grades are far more likely to be receptive to modifying their maladaptive behavior than those who feel "oppressed" by the admonitions of their parents, teachers, and resource specialists.

Activities and Exercises

Examining How Someone Else Studies

Student Book page 47

Identifying the Specifics

Student Book page 48

Evaluating the Identified Study Procedures

Student Book page 48

Predicting What Will Happen

Student Book page 49

After reading the introductory anecdote, students examine Kenesha's study *modus operandi*, identify her specific counterproductive study behaviors, evaluate her decisions, and predict the possible and probable effects of her study procedure on her grades, her ability to concentrate, and her relationship with her parents and teachers. The exercises reinforce a fundamental academic cause-and-effect principle: Conscientious, focused, and efficient work produces enhanced performance. This key principle is a thematic thread woven into every unit.

Defending a Position

Student Book page 49

This activity asks students to list hypothetical rationalizations and justifications that Kenesha might use to justify her studying *modus operandi*. It also asks students to project what issues would likely concern Kenesha's parents. The exercise presents both sides of the issue of efficient versus inefficient studying.

After considering the pros and cons, students make suggestions about how Kenesha might improve her study environment and her homework efficiency. In so doing, they apply what they have learned so far about studying more effectively. The goal is for them to gain insight by analyzing another student's counterproductive behavior and to apply these insights in improving their own study procedures

In the final component of the exercise, students create their own personalized study procedure. Resistance is defused because the study plan reflects the insights that they themselves acquired through their critical assessment of Kenesha's flawed study procedures.

Doing Several Things at Once

Student Book page 51

This exercise is designed to heighten your students' awareness about the likely negative consequences of trying to do more than one thing at a time. The activity underscores the basic cause-and-effect link between concentration and achievement. Students then evaluate a range of hypothetical school-related scenarios that are intended to reinforce the value of good organization.

Creating Your Own Study Fortress

Student Book page 53

Students are encouraged to create a study environment that is a quiet and peaceful "fortress." This metaphor is intended to create and imprint a positive visual association with having an organized study environment free from distractions. The activity guides students to the realization that they can control the conditions in their study fortress, and clearly underscores the benefits of deliberate self-regulation.

What's Right in This Picture?

Student Book page 54

Students critically analyze an illustration that depicts a study environment that is organized and conducive to studying. They identify the factors responsible for the student's productive studying and make predictions about the consequences. The activity reinforces the organizational principles that are examined in the unit.

What's Wrong in This Picture?

Student Book page 56

Students critically analyze an illustration that depicts a study environment that is disorganized and non-conducive to studying. Students identify the factors responsible for the student's non-productive studying and make predictions about the consequences. The exercise further reinforces the organizational principles that are examined in the unit.

Ideas for Reducing Distractions When You Study

Student Book page 57

Students make a list of specific ideas for creating more order in their study environment. This exercise offers them an opportunity to summarize and apply what they have learned about ways to enhance their homework *modus operandi*.

Experimenting with Reducing Distractions

Student Book page 58

Plotting Your Progress

Student Book page 60

Students apply their ideas during a two-week experiment to determine if an enhanced study environment can improve their school performance. Ideally, the effects of their intentional reduction of distractions will translate into improved homework and test grades. Obviously, struggling students also need to acquire a range of specific academic skills enhancements before significant improvement in their grades can be realistically expected. These enhancements will be introduced in subsequent units. The objective of this activity is for students to come to the realization that better organization and improved study habits will produce enhanced academic achievement.

Until students can demonstrate that they are consistently applying the distraction-reducing methods that have been taught, they should continue to track their performance and plot their progress. Improved grades, affirmation, praise, and encouragement are the most powerful catalysts for modifying the counterproductive attitudes and behavior of students who are struggling with learning differences. Achievement is habit forming, and once students taste it, they usually want more.

Teaching Notes

Unit 5: Having a Master Plan

Objectives:

This unit provides your students with opportunities to review, practice, apply, and assimilate the efficient study principles introduced in the preceding units.

Basic Lesson Plan

Student Book pages 65-68

Appendix page 114 - Keeping Track of My Performance
            page 115 - My Personal Performance Chart
            page 116 - Keeping Track of My Performance

1.   Students read **COVERING EVERY BASE** and learn about Andrew's study strategy and his methods for dealing with his anxiety.

2.   In **PUTTING THE PLAN INTO ACTION,** students analyze Andrew's study plan and his techniques for dealing with stress. They then brainstorm additional ideas that might improve his test-preparation procedures and test performance.

3.   In **DEVELOPING YOUR OWN MASTER STUDY PLAN,** students do a two-part strategic studying experiment. In Part One, they check off the studying techniques they have used for the day, and in Part Two, they apply all of the study techniques, keep track of their performance for two weeks, and measure their improvement. This experiment is intended to link and reinforce the efficient study skills they have learned in the first section of the book.

Making Effective Study Procedures a Habit

Assimilating any significant new skill requires effective instruction, repeated opportunities to practice, and recognition of the benefits that can be derived from mastering the skill. The dynamics of this assimilation process are especially relevant when students are learning how to study more efficiently.

The objective is for your students to use productive study habits *automatically* whenever they are faced with academic obligations, such as completing homework assignments or studying for tests that require focused effort, careful planning, and self-discipline. This unit affords another opportunity for students to apply, reinforce, and assimilate what they have learned about organization, scheduling, recording assignments, and creating a conducive study environment.

Activities and Exercises

Putting the Plan into Action

Student Book page 66

This activity has two goals: to provide a quick review of previously taught study techniques and to demonstrate to students that they have acquired a range of practical skills that can help them achieve in school. This realization will build their academic self-confidence and ideally motivate them to apply consistently what they have learned to date.

Developing Your Own Master Study Plan

Student Book page 67

In this section, students again apply and reinforce their strategic planning and organizational skills. They practice methodically checking off the requisite steps for studying efficiently and effectively, and they initiate an experiment in which they apply all of the techniques they have learned and keep track of their performance for two additional weeks. The goal for the students is to continue using the study techniques and to get into the habit of continuously monitoring their performance.

Part 2

Power-Charging Your Studying

Teaching Notes

Unit 6: Power-Reading

Objectives:

This unit teaches students how to speed-read, mind-map, identify and organize important information, improve reading comprehension, and increase retention.

Basic Lesson Plan

Student Book pages 70 - 83

Appendix page 117 - Sample Mind-Map
page 118 - Completed Mind-Map

1. After reading the introductory anecdote, students learn the six steps to effective mind-mapping.

2. Students learn how to speed-read and practice the technique.

3. Students use the mind-mapping method with a typical science unit, compare their mind-maps with a sample, identify the information they have omitted, and expand their mind-maps. They have the option of creating a traditional mind-map or, if they prefer, an artistic mind-map (a sample is included). If appropriate, they recopy their mind-map to improve neatness, legibility, and organization.

4. Students use their mind-map to answer the title question they posed before reading and mind-mapping the unit. They then complete a quick review of the mind-mapping steps.

5. *Optional assignment:* To reinforce mastery, students ask a main-idea question, speed-read, and mind-map using a unit from one of their own textbooks.

The Reading-Skills Hierarchy

During the first years of elementary school, remedial-reading instruction focuses primarily on helping students master the fundamentals: auditory and visual discrimination, phonics, word attack, blending, tracking, common sight-word recognition, and basic reading comprehension. Teaching students how to decipher letters and words accurately, however, is only one step in the process of acquiring good reading skills. Students must also be able to comprehend the words they are reading.

Most students progress from deciphering letters and words to acquiring higher-level comprehension skills with relatively little difficulty. For those struggling with learning differences, however, this transition can be very painful. These students are often so depleted by their efforts to decode that they have little energy left to understand what the words actually mean.*

Addressing the perceptual processing deficits of struggling students and providing specialized learning assistance that initially focuses on basic decoding skills is unquestionably a pedagogically sound instructional strategy. These fundamentals must be taught and mastered *before* LD students can realistically be expected to understand what they are reading

As children advance beyond second grade, the focus of mainstream classroom reading instruction begins to shift. Decoding skills are, of course, still emphasized in grades three through six, but students are now required to understand, retain, and apply the content of what they read. This shift from basic perceptual decoding to the *utilization* of information is reflected in textbooks that become increasingly cognitive as children progress into the upper grades.

On the most basic level of reading comprehension--the **literal level**--the retention of information is emphasized. Students are expected simply to remember what they have read.

Literal Level: The boy picked up the toy sailboat and carried it to the pond.

Literal Question: What did the boy do?

On the second level of reading comprehension--the **inferential level**-- information is implied, but not stated. Students are expected to draw conclusions and make deductions.

Inferential Level: The boy picked up the toy sailboat and carried it to the pond.

Inferential Question: What do you think he was going to do?

---

* There are exceptions. Some students with poor decoding skills are miraculously able to comprehend what they are reading despite chronic decoding inaccuracies. These children are typically very intelligent and are able to compensate successfully for their perceptual dysfunction.

On the highest level of comprehension--the **applicative level**-- students are expected to utilize information.

Applicative level: The boy picked up the toy sailboat and carried it to the pond.

Applicative Question: What might you want to take with you if you were going with the boy?

By the time students enter middle school, teachers require that they be able to answer questions that gauge their retention and understanding of what they are reading on all three levels of comprehension. The process of teaching them to apply and evaluate critically the content in their textbooks accelerates in high school. Students who can comprehend, recall, infer, distill, synthesize, and apply what they read are rewarded with good grades and are on a track leading to college and more challenging, satisfying, and remunerative careers. Conversely, those who do not have first-rate comprehension skills are at risk for discovering that the doors to higher education and professional careers are blocked.

In upper-level classes, and especially accelerated, college-oriented classes, the capacity to memorize historical facts, scientific formulas, and math equations does not necessarily guarantee good grades. The teachers of advanced courses require that students also be able to analyze and critically evaluate what they are learning. Demanding insight, teachers want their students to be capable of interpreting information and ferreting out the underlying issues, themes, and implications. Students who possess superior analytical thinking skills and those who can express their thoughts and feelings cogently and persuasively are generally rewarded with the best grades

Many publishers and educators consider the current emphasis on developing critical-thinking skills innovative. With great pride, they point out that material expressly designed to develop critical intelligence is being incorporated into textbooks at the elementary, middle, and secondary levels. These claims of innovation are ironic given that systematic procedures for methodically training students to think analytically were first introduced more than twenty-five-hundred years ago by Socrates, Plato, and Aristotle.

There are obvious explanations for the reading comprehension and analytical thinking deficiencies of special education students. Struggling to keep up with their mainstream classes and preoccupied with mastering basic reading, math, and expository-writing skills, the overriding priority for most LD students is academic survival. Relatively few acquire the ability to *think and learn actively.* Most haven't a clue about how to identify, evaluate, retain, and apply information and concepts. For these struggling students, studying translates into little more than a mindless procedure of turning the pages of their textbooks while they watch a favorite sitcom or listen to loud music.

To acquire good reading-comprehension and analytical-thinking skills, special education students must be systematically taught how to:

- **identify important information**

- **differentiate main ideas from details**

- **recognize and comprehend key concepts**

- **understand and critically evaluate underlying issues**

- **retain facts**

- **apply what they have learned**

In subsequent units, your students will learn different methods for attaining these objectives, and they will learn and practice a range of comprehension-enhancing methodologies that incorporate different learning styles and preferences. The objective is for them to select a learning strategy or combination of strategies that works for them and enhances their learning efficiency and effectiveness.

Mind-Mapping

Mind-mapping (also referred to as "chunking") is an engaging method for organizing and representing information so that students can better understand, recall, and use the information. This visually-oriented technique encourages students to think about how ideas and facts are linked. Since most students find mind-mapping enjoyable and easy to learn, the method encourages them to become more actively involved in the reading/learning process. The net result of this active learning typically is improved comprehension and retention.

Once students master the mind-mapping method, they can modify the procedure so that it conforms to their own personal learning style and the requirements of the subject matter. In the Unit 7, a more traditional note-taking system is introduced. Although some students may prefer this traditional system, you should encourage them to experiment with mind-mapping. They may discover that the technique works for them and has application in many different learning contexts.

Activities and Exercises

Learning a Method for Studying More Effectively

Student Book page 73

The first step in mind-mapping is for students to transform the title of the material into a main-idea question. They then take a few moments to think about what they may already know about the subject before they begin to speed-read or skim the material. (Many students are quite surprised to realize that they actually know a great deal about the subject they're studying!)

Learning How to Speed-Read

Student Book page 74

Students are now ready to speed-read the unit. There are two objectives for this step:

1. **to learn how to acquire a quick overview of the content**

2. **to become aware of how the key information is linked**

Before students attempt to speed-read the unit, demonstrate how to use two fingers as a governor when skimming. (See illustration on page 74 of student edition). Stress the importance of moving their fingers quickly from left to right across the lines of text. It is also important to emphasize that they should not sound out each word. As special education students have been methodically trained to read word-by-word and pronounce (or sub-vocalize) the words in their minds, this procedure may be difficult for them, and they may be initially resistant to speed-reading. The antidote is to convey enthusiasm and make learning the new procedure fun. It is important to create a *"let's learn this new technique together and see if it works for you"* context.

Discuss with your students what they have learned from speed-reading the unit. As this represents a new skill, you cannot realistically expect them to have retained very much. The goal is for them simply to have a better general idea of the content. If they retain nothing, you may want them to speed-read the unit a second time.

Emphasize that when students scan, they simply want to get a sense of the key ideas. They will need to practice this method repeatedly, and you will need to monitor them to ensure that they're using the technique properly. The scan should take no more than *one minute per page*.

If a student's decoding skills are still very weak and if scanning generates too much stress, you can, of course, eliminate the speed-reading step and proceed directly to mind-mapping. (It's possible that your students already know how to mind-map, as this method is taught in many schools). If this is the case, you can use this unit for review and skill enhancement.

Practicing Mind-Mapping

Student Book page 77

Before beginning their mind-map, have your students briefly examine and discuss the sample mind-map (student book page 78) so that they have an idea of what they are expected to do. You can have them put the sample away and continue mind-mapping on their own, or you can allow them to use the sample as a guide for their own mind-map.

The sample mind-map only covers information from the first three paragraphs of the laser unit. While students are doing their mind-maps, you might want to copy this sample (see Appendix) on the chalkboard, leaving plenty of room to add information.

After students have completed mind-mapping the unit, have them discuss what information to add to the sample mind-map of the first three paragraphs that you've copied on the chalkboard. This should be information they have included in their own maps. You might ask students to go to the chalkboard and add this information.

Be supportive of their first effort at mind-mapping. Students' skills will improve with practice and guidance. Your enthusiasm and affirmation will determine their receptivity, stimulate their effort and motivation, and enhance their self-confidence. Your goal is for students to develop an *"I can do this!"* mindset.

Some students will be able to complete their mind-maps with very little instruction. Others will need more help. Depending on your students' skill level, you may find it expedient to continue mind-mapping the entire unit on the chalkboard and demonstrate step-by-step how the material should be mapped. Discuss why certain information should be included or not included. Make the procedure fun!

Mind-maps do not have to be uniform. Key data should be recorded and linked so that it makes sense, and there is a great deal of latitude. Encourage students to develop their own individual creative style. *The goal is to make the process enjoyable and provide a resource students will want to use.*

If you observe that the students are confused about how to connect the data or do not understand the material, re-examine the material together. Be patient and sensitive. You may need to model again how to do the map, or you may actually need to help them complete the mind-map. Your overriding objective is to demonstrate that there are threads that link ideas and data. By helping students perceive these connections, you are helping them enhance their comprehension and retention.

For many students, imprinting a visual image can be an important memory jogger. This is, of course, especially true in the case of visual learners. These students may not intuitively realize that the visual modality is their best learning mode. Experimenting with mind-mapping may literally be an "eye-opener" and reveals recall abilities students did not realize they possessed.

Encourage students to make designs and artistic embellishments around the data that are as intricate as they want. This can make the process more enjoyable. Creativity stimulates active thinking and enhances comprehension and retention. Remind students to abbreviate whenever possible, but be sure to stress that it's essential that they be able to read their own mind-map!

Reviewing and Completing the Mind-Mapping Steps
Student Book page 81
Step 6: Answering the Title Question
Student Book page 81

This activity encourages students learn how to summarize what they've read. You should allow them to use their mind-maps to answer the question and discourage them from referring back to the unit. Your goal is for students to appreciate how much they've learned about lasers by doing the mind-map. You also want them to discover that learning in this way can be fun.

Your students will be using the same facsimile science unit in the next unit, and they will learn a great deal more about lasers by the time they complete the "Chewing-Up Information" activities presented in Unit 7. At this point, do not expect their answers to the main-idea question to be comprehensive. The primary objective is for students to write an effective and convincing short essay that presents an overview of what they've learned so far. An equally important secondary goal is to build your students' confidence in their ability to express their ideas and insights in written language. They will have many more opportunities to write essays in subsequent units.

This writing exercise is intended to impress upon students the importance of *thinking about* what they are reading and to demonstrate how much can be learned and retained by mind-mapping. The exercise is also intended to improve language-arts skills by giving students an opportunity to write a didactic essay after having assimilated information about a subject. In subsequent units, specific activities will model how to write powerful topic and concluding sentences and how to organize essays so that they are cogent and persuasive.

<u>Teaching Notes</u>

Unit 7: Powering Up Your Reading Comprehension

<u>Objectives:</u>

This unit teaches students another system for improving their comprehension, retention, and application skills. This easy-to-use method for "digesting" information in textbooks is an alternative to the mind-mapping technique introduced in Unit 6.

<u>Basic Lesson Plan</u>

Student Book pages 85-99

Appendix page 119 - Lasers: Expanding the Frontiers of Science and Technology

1. After reading **CONFRONTING A DISASTER**, students examine Wyatt's options when he receives an unexpected poor grade on a test.

2. Students learn how their brain assimilates information when they are reading. This explanation is intended to prepare them for the introduction of a more comprehensive study procedure called the **"Chewing-Up Information" Method.** They discover that they have already learned Step 1 of the system in Unit 6: *Turn the title into a main-idea question.* They are taught the *main-idea question words* and the *detail question words.* They practice turning a series of titles into main idea questions, and they also practice figuring out titles from questions.

4. Students learn and practice steps 2-4 of the **"Chewing-Up Information" Method.** They turn each subtitle of the laser article into *Main-Idea Questions.* They then speed-read the section once again (Step 3) and examine a sample of underscored key information in paragraphs 1-3. Once they understand how to identify important facts, they practice either highlighting or underlining the entire laser section. They then answer the subtitle questions they posed in Step 2 using the highlighted unit and their mind-maps.

5. Students take a practice quiz that will ideally demonstrate how much they have learned about lasers using mind-mapping and the **"Chewing-Up Information" Method.**

6. Students critically examine their performance on the quiz and, if appropriate, identify possible reasons that might explain why they have not done as well as they would have liked. Students are advised that in subsequent units they will learn additional study procedures that can further improve their comprehension, recall, and test performance.

7. The final activity is designed to help students appreciate that **mind-mapping** and the **"Chewing-Up Information" Method** are overlapping resources that can and should be used in tandem to enhance their learning efficiency.

Digesting Important Information

Some underachieving students work diligently, but their efforts prove unproductive because they do not know how to engage themselves actively when they study. The effects of their passive involvement are predictable: marginal comprehension, substandard test performance, and poor grades.*

Intellectual and academic passivity can be an unfortunate by-product of prolonged learning assistance.   One of the obvious primary objectives of special education teachers is to help struggling students handle the demands of the curriculum and survive academically. At the same time, there is a major risk associated with intensive remediation: Students with chronic learning problems may become excessively dependent, both intellectually and emotionally, on those assisting them.

Resource specialists and special-day-class teachers walk a tightrope. If they provide too much help, they can discourage independent thinking and learning. If they provide too little help, their students are at risk for becoming frustrated and demoralized. Determining what constitutes too much assistance and what constitutes too little assistance can pose a major dilemma for special education professionals. Each student's needs must be assessed both objectively and subjectively. In the final analysis, the appropriate amount of assistance that should be provided hinges on the experience, intuition, and judgment of the resource specialist.

---

* **The continual struggle to process, associate, and retain information can be profoundly demoralizing. Learning differences can undermine the desire to learn and exhaust the struggling student's resolve. Before LD students can realistically be expected to become motivated and intellectually engaged, their learning deficits must be identified and effectively addressed.**

Dependency and intellectual and academic passivity are, unfortunately, habit-forming. Students who become addicted to thinking, studying, and learning passively and mindlessly must be guided to an important insight: Academic achievement requires focused effort and active involvement in the studying process. Resource specialists must continually emphasize this cause-and-effect link, and they must teach students how to "digest" the content of their textbooks so that they can understand, assimilate, recall, and apply the information they are studying.

The first step in helping students become more fully engaged learners is to train them to ask incisive questions as they read and study. The next step is to teach them how to identify important information and how to use this information to answer the questions they have posed.

Activities and Exercises

Confronting a Disaster

Student Book page 85

The introductory anecdote describes a highly motivated student who experiences a setback when taking a test. Students are asked to evaluate the student's dilemma and consider how he might avoid a similar setback in the future. The activity is intended to guide students to the realization that to avoid another catastrophe, Wyatt must:

1. **assess what happened**
2. **identify the factors that caused the setback**
3. **evaluate his options**
4. **anticipate the possible and probable consequences of each option**
5. **decide how best to proceed**

Your students have undoubtedly experienced similar setbacks in their own lives, and they should find the anecdote very relevant. As they analyze Wyatt's situation, you want them to recognize that if Wyatt thinks strategically and rationally, he can develop a more productive study procedure, and he can significantly reduce the likelihood of experiencing a similar reversal in the future. This critically important insight is vital if students are to begin assuming responsibility for themselves and their academic performance.

Weighing the Options

Student Book page 86

Students examine three possible responses to receiving a poor grade and consider the probable consequences. By having them analyze another student's setback, they are guided to the realization that there are alternatives to becoming demoralized and academically dysfunctional.

When confronted with a reversal, LD students often react defensively and blame others, rationalize or make excuses such as: "The test was unfair!" "The teacher asks dumb questions!" "I'm just stupid!" These responses, which are clearly designed to cope with failure, shift the onus of responsibility and discourage proactive problem-solving.

Setbacks are an escapable fact of life. The objective is for students to recognize that most problems can be resolved if they carefully and objectively analyze the situation, identify the causal factors, and develop a reasonable, practical, solution-oriented strategy. (Specific methods for solving problems are examined in depth in the final section of this book.)

How the Brain Works When You Read

Student Book page 87

In this exercise, students are asked to think about what happens inside their head when they read and study. For many students, the explanation may trigger their first conscious consideration of how their brain actually responds to the words that they read.

The "Chewing-Up Information" Method

Student Book page 88

Successful students realize that effective studying involves more than simply reading words. To achieve academically, they must also carefully consider what the words mean.

The **"Chewing-Up Information" Method** shows students how to engage themselves intellectually. The method trains them to ask questions and teaches them how to identify, understand, and recall important information.

Students systematically practice each step of the method. Once they assimilate the first four steps, mastery should be reinforced by having students practice the method with content from one of their textbooks. You may, however, prefer that they do the supplemental exercise first.

Asking students to underline or highlight in this workbook is, of course, risky. Students might construe this as a license to underline or highlight in all of their textbooks. The procedure is used here to demonstrate how to identify and extract key data when reading and is a precursor to taking notes. Emphasize that highlighting is permitted only in this workbook. In Unit 8, your students will learn how to transfer key information directly to their notes without having to mark up their textbooks.

You can significantly reduce resistance to the **"Chewing-Up Information" Method** if you help students recognize that the system can significantly improve their grades. Students who have struggled in school and who have low academic self-confidence will obviously require extra help in mastering the procedure. Re-orienting their attitudes about themselves and their abilities is vital. The goal is for students to see themselves as actually being capable of achieving academically. Before this shift in mind-set can be realistically achieved, students will require tangible proof that they are making progress and that their newly acquired study skills are, in fact, having a positive impact on their performance. Resistance to acquiring and using the new study methods should be lessened, and your students' self-confidence and motivation should demonstrably improve.

Learning More Steps to the "Chewing-Up Information" Method
Student Book page 90

Student practice posing key questions as they study, and they also practice answering these questions incisively and succinctly. The methodical procedure of answering the subtitle questions is designed to help them acquire vital expository-writing skills. The activity requires that students understand the information they have studied and that they be able to express their understanding in writing. Language-arts skills must be developed systematically and sequentially, and practice and feedback are vital. Examine and discuss your students' answers to the questions. If you observe run-on sentences or poor syntax and grammar, you will obviously want to work with your students on rephrasing their answers. Resist the temptation to have students correct or revise every mistake. This could turn them off and cause them to become resistant. The goal is to help students improve incrementally their ability to summarize and distill key information.

In this section, students also practice highlighting key information. As previously discussed, this is a preliminary step to learning how to take traditional notes.

A Practice Quiz

Student Book page 96

This quiz will ideally demonstrate that The **"Chewing-Up Information" Method** has significantly enhanced learning. Some questions on the test are quite difficult, and your students will have to use logic to eliminate incorrect answers to deduce the correct ones.

Quiz answers: 1. E 2. T 3. T 4. F 5. F 6. A 7. C 8. C 9. A 10. F 11. F

12. Light Amplification by Stimulated Emission of Radiation

13. **Possible answers include:** recording music   reading bar codes   storing computer disks   making movies   tracking satellites   aiming weapons   welding circuits   telephone or TV fiber optics   making holograms   measuring distance   surgery

Examining How You Did on the Quiz

Student Book page 98

Students who have difficulty with the test will need to be reassured that with sufficient practice using their new study methods, their test performance will improve. It would be a good idea to have students who did poorly review what they have highlighted. Ask them to summarize verbally the important information they have identified. If the test or the discussion reveal that they have omitted important information, have them go back to the laser sections and highlight the missing information. (Please note: Specific techniques for memorizing key facts are presented in Unit 9.) Once students who struggled with the test have reviewed and discussed the key information, have them retake the quiz. The objective is for them to do well and be motivated to learn methods that can improve their comprehension and test performance and build their self-confidence. Once they are certain the system can produce positive payoffs, they will be more predisposed to use the methods.

True/False Answers: 1. T 2. F 3. F 4. T 5. F 6. T 7. T 8. F 9. T 10. T 11. T 12. T

In the following units, students will have further practice using the **"Chewing-Up Information" Method** and will learn the more traditional note-taking method. They can then decide which method works best for them.

<u>Teaching Notes</u>

Unit 8: Taking Notes

<u>Objectives:</u>

This unit teaches your students how to identify important information, take effective notes in standard form, differentiate main ideas from details, and write powerful short essays that demonstrate comprehension of what has been studied.

<u>Basic Lesson Plan</u>

Student Book pages 101-118

Appendix page 122 - Cleopatra: One of the Most Fascinating Queens in History

1. Students read **PREPARING FOR A TEST.** They review the first four steps of the **"Chewing-Up Information" Method** and, after studying an expanded list of common abbreviations, they convert the information they have already highlighted in unit 7 into standard note form. They then complete taking notes on the entire laser unit.

2. Students use the first four steps of the **"Chewing-up Information" Method** in preparing a facsimile history unit about Cleopatra. They begin by copying a small section of sample notes, and they continue taking notes on the unit on their own and without highlighting or underlining. They then compare their notes with model notes and examine similarities, differences, and problems they encountered.

3. Students study model topic sentences and concluding sentences. Using these models as guidelines, they write answers to the *subtitle* (main-idea) questions about the Cleopatra unit that they posed before they began taking notes. They then write a "thumbnail outline" before answering the *title* (main-idea) question. Finally, they compare their essay answers with model essays.

4.   In **DISTINGUISHING MAIN IDEAS FROM DETAILS**, students learn how to review effectively when studying their notes before a test.   They color-code information in their notes to differentiate main ideas from details and learn how to transfer this information to index cards that they can use to review for tests. To reinforce the study methods they have learned, they complete two "What I Have Learned" checklists.

Coasting in Mental Neutral

Many LD students haven't a clue about how to identify, digest, extract, distill, link, and recall the important information in their textbooks.   When asked how they would study for a history or science test, they typically respond: "I guess I might re-read the stuff in the textbook."

There are, of course, a plethora of plausible reasons why students with learning problems study ineffectually and do poorly on tests.   Many who continually struggle in school are discouraged and demoralized.   Some are depleted by their efforts to decode language.   Some cannot concentrate.   Some are unmotivated and psychologically defended because the obstacles they face appear insurmountable. Some are in the habit of choosing the path of least resistance and doing the minimum possible.   Others have never been methodically taught, or have failed to assimilate, the basic nuts and bolts of productive studying and effective learning.

Students who learn passively may go through the motions of studying, but the process is mechanical.   Studying usually translates into a thoughtless process of turning pages in their textbooks. Their brain is on automatic pilot, and there is virtually no cognition or retention. The goal is simply to finish their homework as quickly as possible so that they can do other things. Wanting to avoid anything that requires additional time and effort, they relegate comprehension, recall, and content mastery to the bottom of their list of priorities.

Achieving students have very different priorities and a very different *modus operandi*. These students typically study with their brain fully engaged. They:
- **think about what they are learning**
- **identify key information**
- **ask questions about the content until they understand the information**
- **relate what they are currently learning to what they have already learned**
- **differentiate main ideas from details**
- **take notes and systematically review their notes when they prepare for tests**

- **develop a system for remembering important information**
- **anticipate what the teacher is likely to ask on the next quiz or test**

Successful students realize that taking notes can help them understand and recall what they are studying. They also recognize that note-taking can help them target, extract, understand, and retain the important information that their teachers expect them to learn.

Some mainstream classroom teachers assume that students will intuitively figure out on their own how to take notes. This is wishful thinking. Most students in special education are not intuitive learners. These struggling learners need to be taught how to identify and record information efficiently.

Other teachers believe that they can teach note taking by simply requiring their students to copy notes from the chalkboard. Although this robotic procedure does provide a model for note-taking and ensures uniformity, the method discourages active learning. In effect, the teacher does all the thinking and distilling. The procedure is not only boring, it is also mind-dulling. A far more effective alternative is to teach students an organized system for taking notes and to help them realize that note-taking is their ally when they study, not their enemy.

Students should ideally begin learning how to take notes in fourth grade. They may complain that note-taking requires extra time, and this is certainly true, but the potential benefits of their learning how to take notes are incontrovertible. Of course, other legitimate academic priorities must take precedence in the case of students who learn differently. Academically-deficient students must first learn how to decode sensory data more efficiently, read and comprehend at grade level, and write more effectively. These compelling basic scholastic necessities notwithstanding, LD students must also be taught how to study effectively if they are ultimately to be successfully integrated into mainstream classes.

The key objective of this unit is to guide students to the realization that note-taking can ultimately reduce the total amount of time required to study effectively for tests.

Instead of having to re-read entire chapters, they can review their notes and immediately access the important information. This can be a vital resource when they are faced with midterms or finals in many different subjects.

Activities and Exercises

Learning How to Take Notes

Student Book page 102

In Unit 7 the procedure of underlining or highlighting key information was introduced. This procedure of identifying what is important is a key precursor to learning how to take notes.

In this exercise, students review the first four steps of the **"Chewing-Up Information" Method.** They refer back to the facsimile textbook unit about lasers and discover that the key information they have already highlighted can be easily converted into notes. After examining sample notes on the first section of the laser unit, students transfer the information they underlined or highlighted in Unit 7 into standard note-taking form. They then complete taking notes on the entire laser unit *without* highlighting or underlining the text.

Highlighting or underlining can be a very valuable study procedure, but for obvious reasons students are not usually permitted to mark in their textbooks. Instead of highlighting, they must learn how to identify and underscore important information mentally before transferring the information into notes.

Mastery: More Practice Note-Taking

Student Book page 106

In this exercise, students use the **"Chewing-up Information" Method** to take notes on a facsimile history unit about Cleopatra. The activity reinforces the skills they have learned in the preceding exercise and provides an additional opportunity to practice the note-taking procedure.

After speed-reading the material and writing down main- idea questions from the title and subtitles, students begin to take notes. When they finish, they compare their notes to the sample notes found on page 109. For additional practice, you might have them take notes on an actual section in one of their textbooks.

Answering Essay Questions

Student Book page 111

Answering Subtitle Questions

Student Book page 112

Answering the Title Question

Student Book page 113

After studying model topic and concluding sentences, students use their notes to answer the subtitle questions. They then make a quick "thumb-nail" outline of the important information in the unit and use the outline to answer the title question.

When students finish their essays, have them compare what they have written to the model essays on page 115. Discuss any difficulties they encountered in writing the essays.

Explain that the model essays are a standard toward which they can aim and that their writing skills will improve with practice. The important elements to underscore include:

- **Having a powerful topic sentence**
- **Having a powerful concluding sentence**
- **Including important facts**
- **Organizing information**
- **Proofreading to find careless mistakes**

Distinguishing Main Ideas from Details

Student Book page 116

In this exercise, students go through their notes and color-code the main ideas and details with two different-colored highlighters, pencils, or felt pens. Main ideas might, for example, be highlighted in orange and details in yellow or blue. The main ideas need to be understood, and the supporting details need to be memorized. This color-coding procedure is designed to help students target what they need to learn and enhance their comprehension of the content. Visibly identifying the main ideas and details in their notes can be an invaluable asset during the final review before a test.

Having students write the main ideas on one side of an index card and the relevant details on the other side can be of value when they prepare for tests. Because the information is accessible, students could review the index cards before a test or in a study hall.

In the last activity, students complete two inventories that review the study techniques they have learned about using the "Chewing-Up Information" Method, taking notes, and answering main-idea and detail essay questions.

Teaching Notes

Unit 9: Studying for Tests

Objectives:

This unit integrates and amplifies the study techniques taught in previous units and creates a practical format for a methodical and comprehensive test preparation methodology.

Basic Lesson Plan

Student Book pages 119-140

Appendix page 122 – Cleopatra: One of the Most Fascinating Queens in History

1. Students read **DEVELOPING A TEST-PREPARATION STRATEGY** and review the eleven test-preparation steps they have learned for enhancing their study effectiveness. They then add three additional steps to the list. They explore what teachers are likely to consider important when making up a test.

2. Students learn how to use a template for making certain they study effectively. This template is summarized by the acronym **ICRA** --**I**dentify, **C**omprehend, **R**ecall, and **A**nticipate.

3. To encourage students to "think like a teacher" when they study, they practice making up and answering *short- answer/detail questions* about the Cleopatra unit.

4. Students practice making up and answering *true/false questions*.

5.   Students practice making up and answering *multiple-choice questions*.

6. In **WORKING BACK FROM MULTIPLE-CHOICE ANSWERS**, students learn how to eliminate implausible choices when they aren't certain about the correct answer.

7. In **JOLTING YOUR MEMORY,** students learn alternatives to the traditional methods for memorizing important information (i.e., repetitive writing or reciting facts). They learn how to form powerful visual associations and practice the three steps of the

association/visualization technique with a wide range of typical information they might be expected to memorize in school.

8. Students make up their own tests from questions they have posed as the next-to-last step in the studying process. They examine the issue of anticipating what their teacher is likely to ask on a test and then complete a test-preparation checklist that enumerates the study techniques they have learned. The objective is for this checklist to become the final step in their systematic study procedure.

9. In **BEING RELAXED WHEN YOU TAKE TESTS,** students learn several practical methods for reducing their test-taking stress and anxiety.

Devising a Personalized Test-Taking Method

Good test preparation involves more than simply reading the assigned material, taking notes, understanding the content, and identifying important information. Certainly these procedures are important, but two additional equally important procedures are needed to make certain that students study optimally: Students must develop individualized methods for retaining key information that capitalize on their learning strengths and preferred learning modalities, and they must learn how to anticipate the questions teachers are likely to ask on a test.

Most achieving students are on the "same page" as their teachers when they study. They listen for clues about what will be covered on a test. They carefully go over any study guides the teacher hands out. They examine previous tests to identify patterns in the types of questions that are typically asked. Based on this assessment of evidence, they figure out whether the teacher is detail-oriented or concept-oriented, and they then adjust their study procedure accordingly. If they conclude that their teacher is oriented toward details and data, they focus on memorizing facts. If they conclude their teacher is concept-oriented, they focus on understanding issues and identifying concepts. If their teacher wants student to know facts and also understand concepts, strategic students "cover all the bases" when preparing for tests.

Many teachers require students to assimilate and memorize large quantities of information. This might include number facts, historical dates, spelling words, chemical and mathematical formulae, and vocabulary definitions. For some students, memorizing information is relatively easy. For others, and especially those with learning problems, the process can be excruciatingly difficult and painful.

Having difficulty memorizing data in no way impugns the intelligence of students who have a poor memory. These students may not have a natural facility for retaining data, but they may be as bright as or perhaps brighter than students who have better memory skills

Certainly, the capacity to assimilate and recall visual information is critically important. Students are required to remember that 5 X 5 = 25 and that Columbus discovered America in 1492. They are also required to remember that "illustrate" means to draw and that "cultivate" means to grow. These memorization tasks can be especially problematic for students who learn differently, and particularly for those who have auditory and visual memory deficits associated with a perceptual dysfunction.

Students who can recall the visual details (i.e., facts and data) in their textbooks and notes usually do better on information-loaded tests. Because they can "see" words in their mind, they are also usually better spellers. Their visual facility is especially useful with non-phonetic words whose spelling must be memorized. These students know how the word *receive* is spelled because they can visualize it. They don't need to recite the *"i before e except after c"* rule. In contrast, students who are auditory learners typically try to sound out words. The many phonetic exceptions in the English language and the traditional emphasis on data retention in the curriculum place these auditory learners at an academic disadvantage. (It should be noted that auditory learners may be able to capitalize on their preferred learning modality in upper-level classes where a great deal of content is communicated through class discussions and lectures.)

Students, even those who have chronic difficulty memorizing, can be taught highly effective memory techniques that will serve them throughout their lives. They can also be taught how to prepare more strategically for tests by asking and answering questions as they study.

One of the key goals of this program is to teach students how to compensate productively in areas where they lack natural ability. The objective is to provide them with a range of effective study techniques that they can mold into a personalized methodology that works for them.

Activities and Exercises

Learning How to Study Effectively for a Test

Student Book page 120

Passive learners rarely consider the process a teacher follows when making up a test. For these students taking a test is the equivalent playing darts blindfolded. If they're lucky, their darts may occasionally hit the target. Unfortunately, most will probably hit the wall.

This exercise reviews the study techniques that have been presented and explores what teachers might consider important and what they are likely to include on a test. You want students to realize that by preparing strategically, they can improve their grades. You also want them get into the habit of thinking like a teacher as they study. To do so, they must pose questions about the content of what they are learning. This questioning will engage them more actively in the studying process and will improve the likelihood of their anticipating questions that their teachers are probably going to ask on an exam.

A Final Test-Preparation Template

Student Book page 122

This exercise provides your students with a simple acronym--**ICRA**--to help them make certain that they are covering all the bases when studying for exams. The acronym is formed from the four components of the template: **I**dentify (the important information), **C**omprehend (the material), **R**ecall (the facts) and **A**nticipate (what the teacher is likely to ask on a test). In the preceding units, your students have already learned how to identify and comprehend what they are reading. In the subsequent exercises, they will practice making up different types of facsimile test questions, and they will learn methods for memorizing key information.

Making Up and Answering Short-Answer Questions

Student Book page 125

This exercise encourages students to experiment with making up and answering focused questions that address particular facts or details in the material being studied. The procedure underscores the need to identify and "digest" key information and provides opportunities to practice writing concise, cogent sentences that effectively encapsulate important facts.

Making Up and Answering True/False Questions

Student Book page 127

This exercise encourages students to anticipate the type of true/false questions they are likely to encounter on a test. The goal is to hone their tactical planning and encourage them to delve deeply into the content of the material they are studying.

Making Up and Answering Multiple-Choice Questions

Student Book page 128

The objective of this exercise is to encourage students to adjust their study procedures to the specific type of test they expect to take. Your students can anticipate taking many multiple-choice tests during the course of their education, and having the opportunity to practice designing and answering these types of questions will focus their test-preparation procedures, build their self-confidence, reduce their anticipatory anxiety, and improve their grades.

Working Back from Multiple-Choice Answers

Student Book page 130

Students who encounter a multiple-choice question which they cannot immediately answer may simply guess mindlessly. This exercise shows them how to eliminate implausible choices and how to increase their odds of selecting the right answer if they are forced to guess.

Jolting Your Memory

Student Book page 131

Making Powerful Associations

Student Book page 132

This exercise shows your students how to enhance their visualization and memorization skills. It introduces the concept of creating visual images or "hooks" to help them recall important information. By making powerful visual associations and by seeing information in their "mind's eye," they can capitalize on their imagination and creativity to remember spelling, vocabulary definitions, symbols, dates, and number facts.

The technique encourages students to use colored pens or markers to enhance their visualizations, to create vivid images, and to force their eyes into the upper quadrant (visual information is best accessed and represented in this way). This activity requires a great deal of guidance, practice, and monitoring. Once students discover how powerful the methods are, their resistance to being asked to learn something *totally new* should be defused.

Making Up Tests

Student Book page 135

This activity provides students with additional practice thinking like a teacher and anticipating what is likely to be included on a test. Students are asked to make up practice test questions as they study. The goal is to make the procedure of asking questions while studying and when reviewing an integral part of their test preparation. The **Test-Preparation Checklist** encourages students to make certain they have performed all of the steps required to study effectively. This final "countdown" is designed to ensure that they have studied strategically and are fully prepared to take the test. This assurance can significantly reduce students' test anxiety and build their academic self-confidence.

Being Relaxed When You Take a Test

Student Book page 137

Test anxiety can obviously undermine test performance, and the stress and fear can be especially debilitating for students who are struggling academically. In extreme cases, their anxiety, anticipation of disaster, and fear can cause them to become mentally incapacitated. Students who learn differently are particularly vulnerable to "clutching" during tests despite being well-prepared and thoroughly knowing the material. The exercise teaches students several practical, effective, and easy-to-use relaxation techniques that can reduce the debilitating effects of test anxiety.

Part 3

Thinking Smart

Teaching Notes

Unit 10: Problem-Solving

Objectives:

This unit models how problems can be solved when methodically analyzed and broken down into smaller pieces. Students are taught a powerful and easy-to-learn problem-solving method called **DIBS** and are provided with repeated opportunities to practice the method. The scenarios parallel situations and experiences students might encounter in their own lives.

Basic Lesson Plan

Student Book pages 142-150

1. Students read **SURROUNDED BY CHAOS** and then predict the consequences of Paul's behaviors and attitude.
2. In **DIBS: A PROBLEM-SOLVING METHOD,** students use the method to identify and solve Paul's problem.
3. Students apply **DIBS** in solving three additional problems.
4. Students are provided with additional opportunities to practice using with a variety of problems. This reinforcement exercise can be done in class or assigned for homework.

Getting to the Core of a Problem

Students can easily become overwhelmed by problems that appear monumental and insoluble. This is especially true in the case of those who learn differently and who have fragile self-confidence. Many of these struggling students have never developed the analytical thinking skills requisite to assessing problems judiciously and to identifying the underlying issues and causal factors. Because they do not understand why things are "going wrong," they cannot develop a solution-oriented strategy. Their frustration and demoralization magnify their ineffectual problem-solving, and this, in turn, magnifies the frustration and demoralization.

Students who feel inadequate and helpless often latch onto maladaptive behavior to protect themselves from feeling incompetent and vulnerable. This reaction, which typically includes procrastination, irresponsibility, resistance, denial, and blaming, only calls attention to the failings they are trying to hide, but most emotionally vulnerable children are so intent on defending themselves that they do not recognize this irony.

When you systematically teach students how to take a step back from a problem, assess the situation, identify the causative factors, and develop and implement a plan that can resolve the difficulty, you are providing them with an effective alternative to reacting impulsively or mindlessly. Students who learn how to analyze, reason, weigh the pros and cons, and react strategically to predicaments have a monumental advantage over those who act and react without thinking. These students have access to the mental tools they need to handle life's setbacks, challenges, and disappointments. This asset will serve them throughout their lives.

Activities and Exercises

Surrounded by Chaos

Student Book page 142

The introductory anecdote asks your students to examine and analyze another student's counterproductive behavior. Encouraging students to express their reactions and think analytically is vital. Your inclination to provide feedback and direction, however, must be tempered. The goal is for students to deduce on their own which of Paul's behaviors are productive and which are counterproductive. When students express "off-base" or illogical reactions or interpretations, their response must obviously be examined with sensitivity.

This exercise also asks students to make predictions, a key step in the process of training them to consider the potential consequences (i.e., the possible or probable) of their own choices and actions. The predictive procedure underscores the key cause-and-effect principles. These principles will be examined in greater depth in Unit 14.

DIBS: A Problem-Solving Method

Student Book page 144

In this exercise, students use **DIBS** to solve the problem described in the introductory anecdote. The basic premise of the **DIBS** System is that problems become soluble when the "divide and conquer" concept is applied. The first step in the process is to <u>define</u> the problem with precision. Students who focus exclusively on the symptoms of problems and peripheral issues (i.e., "My parents are always picking on me!") cannot come to grips with the underlying factors that are causing the predicament.

DIBS shows students how to break down a problem into manageable pieces and how to develop a solution-oriented strategy. If they use the method properly to analyze Paul's problem and brainstorm solutions, they should produce responses similar to the following:

D(efine) the problem:	Bad attitude and poor organization
I(nvestigate) the causes:	Disorganized desk
	Procrastinates
	Hands in assignments late
	Sloppy work
B(rainstorm) solutions:	Be more organized
	Improve his attitude
S(elect) an idea to try:	Be more organized

The two brainstormed solutions--"be more organized" and "improve his attitude"-- make sense, but they are too general. Steer students toward selecting specific steps that could solve the problem, such as: *Put papers into folders for each subject* or *Make a schedule for doing homework.*

<u>Practicing the DIBS Method</u>

Student Book page 147

Once your students understand **DIBS**, have them use the method to solve these supplemental problems. The extra practice will help them master the procedure. Indicate which problems you want students to do, or let them select the problems. If they are enjoying the process and if there is enough time, they may want to do all the problems.

<u>Mastery: Further Practice with DIBS</u>

Student Book page 149

These problems can be used for additional reinforcement, especially in the case of students who are having difficulty assimilating the procedures. The more students practice, the more likely they will master and use **DIBS.**

Encourage your students to use **DIBS** whenever they have a problem or encounter a difficult challenge in school or outside of school. Sometimes situations occur in class or during an RSP session that offer perfect opportunities for students to apply **DIBS**. You might say, "You told me you are having difficulty completing your math assignments in class. Let's use **DIBS** to examine the problem and find a solution."

Teaching Notes

Unit 11: Goals

Objectives:

This unit guides students to a critically important insight: Establishing short-term and long-term goals is vital to success in any challenging academic or non-academic endeavor. Students are provided with repeated opportunities to practice setting goals and defining the steps required for attaining these objectives. The intent is to make goal-setting second nature.

Basic Lesson Plan

Student Book pages 151-165

Appendix page 125 - A Letter to Myself
page 126 - Weekly Goal Sheet

1. Students read **FIGURING OUT HOW TO GET WHAT YOU WANT**. They discuss the "divide and conquer" process (i.e., breaking problems and challenges down into manageable parts). They examine Brittany's goals, speculate about her feelings of frustration and discouragement, evaluate the strategy she and her father develop to solve the problems, and consider other ideas that might help her achieve her objectives.

2. Students use what they have learned about goal-setting and define their personal long-term and short-goals.

3. Students reinforce goal-setting principles by completing **A LETTER TO MYSELF** in which they enumerate their long- and short-term goals.

4. In **AN EXPERIMENT WITH GOAL-SETTING**, students systematically use the goal-setting principles in their own lives. This activity provides additional practice and is intended to make the process of establishing goals an integral part of students' daily *modus operandi.*

5. Students learn a powerful and effective **4-Part Goal-Setting System** that will help them solve real-world problems they might face in school and at home.

Strategic Thinking

Successful students think strategically. They realize that to get from point A to point D, they must define their overall objective and then focus on attaining specific interim goals along the way. Armed with this navigational system, they systematically proceed through each required station until they ultimately arrive at their destination.

A key trait distinguishes students who think strategically: They intuitively understand or have learned through observation and personal experience that a fundamental and immutable cause-and-effect principle links goal-setting and achievement. This insight shapes their behavior, attitude, judgment, and performance and provides them with a monumental competitive advantage. Strategic students also realize that the payoffs for their tactical, get-the-job-done thinking are greater efficiency, enhanced productivity, and superior achievement, and these rewards more than justify any extra time and effort they may need to invest in attaining their objectives.

Students who are in the habit of thinking strategically define their goals, formulate a pragmatic operational plan, and then focus their intellectual, emotional, and physical energy on getting the job done. They may not necessarily be the brightest in the class, but they typically rank among the highest achievers.

Whereas intelligence is largely inherited, the capacity to think strategically, act smart, and apply intelligence pragmatically is generally acquired through life experience. Strategic students learn from their mistakes, weigh the pluses and minuses, calculate the odds, and devise the most effective and efficient ways to handle challenges. They solve problems, organize their resources, and plan ahead. They carefully consider the potential consequences of their behavior before they act, learn from their mistakes, bounce back from defeat, neutralize obstacles, and figure out how to survive and prevail in a competitive academic arena.

Some students acquire smartness through observation, trial and error, and family modeling. Others need to be taught methodically how to use their brains in much the same way that they need to be taught methodically how to perform a gymnastics routine. The key components in the instructional paradigm are self-evident: a good coach/teacher/parent who can motivate students to develop their natural abilities in tandem with modeling, guided practice, empathic feedback, affirmation, and encouragement.

Most struggling students are preoccupied with basic academic survival, and they may neither recognize nor appreciate the function of goal-setting and strategic thinking in the scholastic-achievement equation. Academically deficient and emotionally fragile students must become convinced that they have a chance of succeeding before teachers and parents can realistically expect them to stretch for demanding goals.

Setting goals can be a double-edged sword for LD students. The student who targets a B in English when his reading and language-arts skills are seriously deficient runs the risk of being thwarted. If he experiences repeated disappointments, his self-concept cannot help but suffer. As the cumulative effect of the disappointments take their toll, the student is likely to become increasingly unmotivated, psychologically defended, and unwilling to risk additional failure. He will then protect himself by retreating into a comfort zone where he has minimal expectations and minimal aspirations.

The strategic-thinking components of this program have been intentionally placed in this final section of the book. At this juncture, your students' academic, study, and test-taking skills have ideally improved. The emphasis now shifts to teaching students how to think more analytically, logically, and strategically. This translates into showing them how to solve problems, develop success-oriented tactics, and establish goals and priorities.

Characteristics of Students Who Think Strategically

1. They set motivational goals. ("I want an A on my science report.")
2. They identify the barriers that stand in the way. ("My handwriting needs to improve.")
3. They assess their options. ("I can go the movies, or I can study for my math test.")
4. They develop a pragmatic plan for getting the job done. ("I must make sure that I have the book report finished by Tuesday so that I can proofread and recopy it on Wednesday and submit it on Thursday.")

Characteristics of Students Who Do Not Think Strategically

1. They have little sense of purpose or direction.

2. They spend inadequate time studying.

3. The do not plan ahead.

4. They are disorganized.

5. They lack motivation.

6. They study and learn passively.

7. They fail to attend to the details.

8. They submit poor quality work.

9. They "forget" to do assignments or submit them late.

10. They misbehave and get in trouble.

11. They don't pay attention in class.

12. They often act in ways that alienate others.

With systematic instruction, most students can significantly improve their ability to think more strategically. By acquiring effective study skills and developing the habit of setting goals, they become the equivalent of heat-seeking missiles that lock onto their target and vector in for the "kill." It doesn't matter whether the target is a touchdown in the next football game or a B+ on the next essay. What does matter is that students get into the habit of striving for personal goals, focusing their efforts, and working to actualize their abilities.

Activities and Exercises

Figuring Out How to Get What You Want

Student Book page 151

Helping students recognize that they are continually making important decisions that affect their lives is step #1 in the process of helping them realize the value of establishing goals. This unit underscores a basic principle in the academic achievement formula: the more astute their decisions, the greater the chances of attaining desirable payoffs.

After reading the introductory anecdote, students examine Brittany's behavior, her frustrations with her playing and with her interactions with her coach, and the plan she and her dad develop to solve the problem. They then brainstorm alternative solutions to the problem.

<u>Checking Out Feelings</u>

Student Book page 154

<u>Solving Problems</u>

Student Book page 155

Struggling, psychologically-defended students often resist examining situations that have caused them emotional pain. To defuse this resistance, these exercises encourage students to examine the feelings someone else is experiencing as she struggles with frustration and discouragement. Asking students to analyze another child's goals, attitudes, and actions allows them to derive insight into themselves and their own *modus operandi* without eliciting defensiveness. Once they realize that the analytical introspective process is not threatening or painful, they will be less resistant to examining their own behaviors, attitudes, and ambitions. The imparted and critically important message is positive and affirming: By strategically analyzing a difficult situation and brainstorming a well-conceived and solution-oriented strategy, most of life's problems can be resolved.

The stage is now set for students to begin analyzing their own *modus operandi*. The sequencing of the exercises is intended to elicit a greater willingness to make constructive changes, think more strategically, and integrate goal-setting into their lives

<u>What Are Your Goals?</u>

Student Book page 155

Before students can fully appreciate the benefits of goal-setting and commit to establishing their own goals, they must become convinced that the procedure can produce desirable payoffs and help them prevail over problems and challenges. The basic premise of this exercise is that LD students can be taught achievement-oriented behaviors.

Students should not be expected to know at the age of 10, or even at the age of 18, what they want to do with the rest of their lives. Goals established during early childhood are often transitory. Some students do maintain their long-term goals, but most change directions many times during their lives.

This exercise is designed to impress upon students the benefits of targeting specific, meaningful personal goals. You want your students to realize that goals provide a sense of direction and purpose, stimulate effort and commitment, and encourage the development of their talents.

A Letter to Myself -- My Goals in School

Student Book page 159

Teaching students that planning and focused effort produce desirable rewards is only one step in training them to think more strategically. Students must also be taught that short-term goals are stepping stones to attaining long-term goals. A child may say that she wants an A in math on her next report card, but she may not have a clue about how to get an A.

This exercise is intended to reinforce once again the cause-and-effect link between establishing motivational goals and attaining desired payoffs. The "Letter to Myself" is designed to serve as a tangible reminder of what students have targeted and what steps they need to take to attain their objectives.

An Experiment with Goal-Setting

Student Book page 160

This activity also reinforces the value of establishing long-term and short-term goals. Emphasize to students that once they get into the habit of focusing on attaining specific objectives, they can do so mentally without having to write their goals down on paper. As the procedure becomes ingrained, students will begin to establish goals *automatically*, and each time they attain a goal, they will replace it with another goal *automatically*.

Using Goals to Solve Problems

Student Book page 161

Students who discover they can use the goal-setting process as a resource for solving problems have a distinct advantage over those who become overwhelmed by problems and mindlessly "spin their wheels." This exercise demonstrates how to use a **4-Part Goal-Setting System** as an alternative to the **DIBS** method in solving a wide range of common in-school and out-of-school conundrums.

Teaching Notes

Unit 12: Priorities

Objectives:

This unit helps students develop the habit of establishing a logical order, determining a hierarchy of importance, and properly sequencing events and lists of items. The activities provide multiple opportunities to practice establishing priorities so that the procedure can be mastered and assimilated.

Basic Lesson Plan

Student Book pages 167-177

1. Students read **FIGURING OUT THE RIGHT ORDER**. They examine the concept of ranking items and events in order of descending or ascending significance.

2. In **LEARNING HOW TO ESTABLISH PRIORITIES**, students revise and re-order Rasheed's list. Some students may require more guidance and supervision than others. (If you are concurrently instructing several homogeneously grouped LD students, you may want to have students work together on the project in a cooperative learning group.) Students then apply the prioritization procedure to ordering the steps involved in writing a term paper.

4. In **ESTABLISHING YOUR OWN PRIORITIES**, students apply and reinforce prioritization principles by renumbering the order of their original **short-term goals** (Student Book page 158). They apply a logical and functional progression that is deliberately designed to facilitate the attainment of their **long-term goals**.

5. In **MASTERY: MORE PRACTICE ESTABLISHING PRIORITIES**, students are provided with another opportunity to master prioritization principles. This exercise can be done in class or assigned for homework.

6. Students examine a plan based upon faulty prioritization and revise the plan.

7. Students then take a quick review quiz to assess whether they understand the concept and application of prioritization procedures.

Creating a Hierarchy of Importance

Students who think strategically realize that if they are to attain their objectives, they must rank their responsibilities and tasks in order of descending or ascending importance. They may not always be consciously aware they are establishing priorities, but they intuitively apply logical and functional ordering principles whenever they are faced with a challenge, problem, or assignment that requires careful strategic planning.

Scholastic success hinges not only on academic skills, effort, and motivation, but also on students being able to figure out what needs to be done, what's most important, and how to sequence tasks and obligations efficiently and effectively. Students must realize that studying for a history test is more important than watching their favorite sit-com on TV. These same prioritization principles are applicable in the world outside of school. If they are packing survival gear on a sailboat, they must recognize that water and food are more important than a walkman, CDs, and games.

Preoccupied with academic survival and intent on defending themselves emotionally, many LD students never learn how to prioritize. They stumble and meander through school without any sense of how to order their responsibilities and get the job done.

Activities and Exercises

Figuring Out the Right Order

Student Book page 167

Most LD students can assimilate prioritizing methods with relative ease. The first step in the process is to demonstrate that methods are *relevant* and *useful*. The introductory story makes this point and clearly underscores the value of setting priorities.

As you teach prioritizing skills, it is important to orchestrate successful experiences for your students. If their logic is "off," you obviously want to help them understand why. You also want to acknowledge that there is usually more than one way to analyze a challenge. You might respond to off-target logic in the following way: "That never occurred to me. What do you think about this alternative way of looking at the situation?" If you have an open mind, you may discover that your student's logic may actually be quite valid.

Establishing Your Own Priorities
Student Book page 171

This activity applies prioritizing skills to a real-life academic situation that your students will encounter in school. They methodically practice applying the functional principles of sequencing events and responsibilities requisite to writing a term paper. You want to encourage your students to apply prioritization procedures in all subject areas. If they are studying about the Civil War in their history class, you could ask them to list the respective strengths of the Union Army and Confederate Army in order of importance to winning the war. You might also ask them to prioritize the requisite steps in writing a book report or to prioritize the strengths of their basketball team. By incorporating prioritizing skills as a strand running through all content areas, you are reinforcing mastery. Once students establish the habit of automatically using these skills, the procedure will become second nature.

Combining Priorities and Goals
Student Book page 172

To complete this exercise, students must refer to an activity they completed on pages 157-158 in Unit 11--**WHAT ARE YOUR GOALS?** The activity provides an opportunity for students to apply prioritization principles to goal-setting.

Mastery: More Practice Establishing Priorities
Student Book page 173

This activity provides additional reinforcement of prioritization, critical thinking, and strategic-thinking principles. The exercise requires that students carefully consider the priorities and provide their rationale for eliminating less essential items from a list of survival gear.

A Plan That Didn't Work

Student Book page 174

This activity encourages critical and strategic thinking. Students analyze another child's mistakes and then modify his priority system so that it is more logical and practical.

What I Have Learned about Priorities

Student Book page 177

Students take a quick review quiz that assesses whether they understand the concept and have mastered and assimilated application of the procedure of establishing priorities.

Answers: T; F; T; F; F; T; T; T; F; F; T; F; F; T

<u>Teaching Notes</u>

Unit 13: Strategies

<u>Objectives:</u>

This unit shows students how to create practical and focused strategies for attaining their goals. The exercises provide repeated opportunities to practice strategic thinking and planning

<u>Basic Lesson Plan</u>

Student Book pages 179-192

Appendix page 127 - My Strategy

1. Students read **GETTING WHAT YOU WANT** and examine the systematic procedures involved in developing a strategy to attain a specific goal. They also practice differentiating long- and short-term goals.

2. Students learn the six key questions they must ask themselves before they can develop an effective strategy, and they then create a plan for helping another student attain her goal of becoming a veterinarian.

3. In **CREATING YOUR OWN STRATEGY** students practice selecting a personal goal and developing a plan for attaining the goal.

4. In **CHANGING COURSE,** students examine whether it is legitimate and justifiable to alter directions after having established a goal and developed a strategy.

5. Students apply strategic-planning concepts in **MASTERY: MORE PRACTICE DEVELOPING STRATEGIES** and develop a plan for solving an environmental problem.

6. Students examine a strategy that is unsuccessful and develop an alternative strategy that can achieve the desired objective.

7. In **REVIEWING WHAT'S SMART AND WHAT'S NOT SMART,** students complete a checklist, apply strategic-thinking principles, and assess the wisdom of a range of behaviors and attitudes

Developing a Plan of Action

Students who can devise a practical plan for getting from point A to point B to point C have a distinct advantage over those who muddle through school with no sense of direction and with no strategy for defining and attaining their personal goals. LD students, and especially those with significant learning differences, are usually preoccupied with making it through the school day with a minimal amount of grief. Most of their physical, intellectual, and emotional energy is devoted to acquiring academic skills, understanding course content, and completing their assignments. Because they are rooted in "present time," they are typically oblivious to the value of defining their goals and creating long-range strategies. The effects are predictable: These students are destined to stumble mindlessly from crisis to crisis without a clue about how to mobilize their efforts productively.

Teaching Students How to Develop Strategies

With proper instruction, all students of normal intelligence can be taught how to think and plan more effectively. To teach them strategic-planning skills, you must be prepared to:

1. **Relate planning procedures to real-life situations** ("How could you organize the project?")
2. **Encourage experimentation with a range of strategies**. ("What could you do to improve your chances of being elected school vice-president?")
3. **Encourage a critical assessment about why some strategies are successful and others are unsuccessful** ("Why do you think the mayor lost his bid for re-election?")
4. **Urge students to search out and analyze strategies in their content area studies** ("Why did the British battle plan during the War of Independence prove ineffective?")
5. **Encourage incorporation of strategic thinking skills into personal planning** ("What steps do you need to take to earn enough money to buy a new computer?)

It is vital that LD students get into the habit of defining their objectives and creating practical strategies for attaining these objectives. To compensate successfully for their learning problems, students must be taught how to develop a plan for getting the job done. They must be able to formulate a strategy for preparing for a final exam or for completing a term paper. The goal is for students to use these planning procedures automatically whenever they are faced with important obligations.

As students become more adept at thinking tactically, their academic performance should improve commensurately. Knowing that they can "attack" challenges and responsibilities analytically, methodically, and strategically will enhance their academic self-confidence and self-reliance and render them more intellectually potent and emotionally resilient. Once they get into the habit of defining their objectives, prioritizing their responsibilities, allocating their resources, and managing their time, they will able to juggle concurrently multiple responsibilities. These might include karate class, soccer practice, daily homework, a weekly vocabulary quiz, a math test, a book report that is due in two days, and a science term paper that is due in two weeks.

The Motivation Factor

Students become motivated when they're convinced that their efforts will produce positive outcomes. Those who enjoy playing basketball and who are certain that they have ability will want to improve their skills. They will practice hard and play hard. As their skills improve, they will become even more motivated. Their effort will produce success, and their success will, in turn, stimulate more effort.

There's an inherent irony in this achievement equation. *To succeed, students must be motivated and willing to work, but in order to be to be motivated and willing to work, they must believe that they can succeed.* Students who lack faith in themselves and their abilities and who do not feel that they can prevail are likely to perform consistently with their negative expectations. They are also at risk for shutting down and accepting marginal performance as their fate. Once they do, they could underachieve throughout their life.

When you teach LD students specific, practical, success-oriented strategies that produce unequivocal evidence of improvement and achievement and when you intentionally structure repeated opportunities for them to experience success, you are playing an instrumental role in helping them alter their negative mindset. Defeated learners who acquire effective skills and who realize that they can actually prevail in school are going to be more motivated and are going to work harder. This diligence in tandem with more efficient study skills will pay lasting dividends in the form of improved grades, enhanced academic self-confidence, and elevated expectations and aspirations.

After your students have completed this unit, urge them to continue establishing goals, setting priorities, planning interim steps, and creating practical strategies for attaining their goals. The objective is for students to apply these planning skills not only in school, but in all aspects of their lives.

Activities and Exercises

Getting What You Want

Student Book page 179

This exercise demonstrates how goal-setting and strategic thinking are linked. Students are asked to examine the procedure that a girl uses to develop a plan for attaining her career goal. Students then create a strategy for another student whose goal is to become a veterinarian. By applying strategic-thinking procedures to another person's challenge, students gain insight without feeling that they themselves are "under a microscope."

Creating Your Own Strategy

Student Book page 184

In this exercise, students use their insights and systematically develop a plan for attaining a personal long-range goal. Once they recognize the practical value and relevance of planning strategically, they will be more predisposed to integrate tactical-thinking procedures into their lives in school and outside of school.

Changing Course

Student Book page 187

This exercise helps students understand that it is OK to abandon a goal that is no longer relevant or no longer works. This is **not** the equivalent of encouraging them to give up when they encounter an impediment, experience a setback, or make a mistake. (These issues are examined in Units 15 and 16.)

Mastery: More Practice Developing Strategies

Student Book page 188

In this exercise, students apply their planning skills and develop a strategy for solving an environmental problem. They use the six key strategic-planning questions introduced in the unit.

A Strategy That Failed

Student Book page 189

This exercise encourages students to look critically at a non-functional strategy and to consider potential flaws, fallacies, and pitfalls in advance. It also encourages them to make expedient modifications in unsuccessful strategies so that they are more effective.

Reviewing What's Smart and What's Not Smart

Student Book page 191

This exercise is designed to encourage introspection and self-assessment. Students are asked to complete a checklist and to evaluate the thinking, attitude, and behavior of other students. This analytical process is designed to be a springboard for them to begin examining their own thinking, attitudes, and behavior.

Teaching Notes

Unit 14: Cause and Effect

Objectives:

This unit teaches students to consider the potential consequences of their decisions and behavior. Students analyze real-world situations and practice predicting outcomes and making judicious choices. The objective is to make thinking about the potential repercussions and implications of their attitudes and behavior an ingrained habit.

Basic Lesson Plan

Student Book pages 193-210

1. Students read **CONSIDERING THE POSSIBILITIES.** They then examine the process of making decisions and dealing with the consequences of these decisions. They list each of Kelsey's decisions, link the decisions with consequences, and evaluate her choices.

2. In **EXAMINING DECISIONS** and **CONSIDERING THE CONSEQUENCES,** the link between choices and outcomes is underscored and reinforced.

3. The concept of a "decision point" is introduced. Students read a short anecdote, identify the decision points, and write down the consequence of each decision. Students indicate whether each consequence is "possible" and "probable" as they assess Evan's choices.

4. Students complete **DESCRIBING A DECISION POINT IN YOUR OWN LIFE.** They identify each decision point in their own story and indicate its consequences.

5. The terminology "cause and effect" is introduced, and in **PRACTICE FIGURING OUT THE EFFECT,** students identify effects and anticipate whether the outcome is possible or probable.

6. In **PRACTICE FIGURING OUT THE CAUSE**, students identify the decisions that are responsible for specific outcomes.

7. In **WHAT WOULD YOU DO?**, students evaluate a range of real-world situations and apply "thinking about the consequences" principles.

8. In **WHAT I HAVE LEARNED ABOUT CAUSE AND EFFECT,** students reinforce what they have learned about consequences and evaluate the smartness of a range of real-life decisions.

Future Thinking

Students who act mindlessly are destined to have repeated painful collisions with the harsh realities of life. If they are to avoid these crashes, they must be trained to consider the potential consequences of their behavior *before* they act. Their success in school and the world outside of school is contingent on their recognizing and assimilating an immutable fact of life: Irresponsibility, procrastination, and marginal effort produce unpleasant outcomes.

The basic premise of this unit is that cognitive behavior-modification methods can be used to help LD students integrate basic cause and effect principles into their daily *modus operandi*. With methodical instructions, sufficient practice, and consistent reinforcement, these students can be conditioned to consider the future implications of their decisions and actions, and in the process, they can acquire the strategic-thinking and planning skills that are requisites to achievement.

LD students must be trained to:
1. consider and apply cause and effect principles
2. evaluate their options and behavior at important "decision points"
3. be conscious of potential outcomes before they commit to an action.
4. factor "future time" (and not just "present time") into the decision making process

The objective is to teach students to think analytically, critically, and strategically when faced with problems and challenges. These attuned students are far more likely to make judicious and well-reasoned choices than those who habitually act impulsively and mindlessly. Students must be methodically guided to the realization that the lack of forethought invariably compounds challenges, deters successful problem-solving, and undermines achievement.

All students will occasionally misjudge a situation, miscalculate the odds, make a mistake, or disregard the predictable implications of their behavior. For example, a student may not study the correct material for a test and may, as a consequence, receive a failing grade. That the student would be upset by the miscue is understandable. If, however, she has been taught to think analytically, she would assess the mistake and do everything possible to avoid repeating it. In the future, she would recheck her assignment sheet to make certain that she has recorded the key information, or she might call a friend to verify what the next test will cover. This capacity to analyze and learn from mistakes differentiates successful students and produces wisdom.

Sometimes, despite careful planning, analytic thinking, and due diligence, things still go awry. Grasping the laws of cause and effect, however, can significantly reduce the incidence of chronic non-judicious behavior that invariably diminishes performance and undermines self-esteem.

Unfortunately, many LD students haven't a clue about how to assess their mistakes and miscalculations, and they are equally clueless about how to use the knowledge derived from these setbacks to guide their future actions. Even bright students may continue to repeat their flawed choices despite obvious predictable consequences. They may talk in class, even though they know that they will be reprimanded. They may hand in late, sloppy, incomplete, or inaccurate work even though they know their behavior will cause them to receive a D or an F. These self-defeating behaviors are the benchmarks of non-strategic thinking.

Every day, students who should know better disregard fundamental cause-and-effect principles. The effects are often disastrous. Students may take unnecessary risks and injure themselves. They may act irresponsibly, misbehave, and get into trouble. They may fail to spend adequate time studying, or if they do study, they may do so thoughtlessly.

Lecturing or punishing students who are oblivious to the consequences of their actions in no way guarantees that they'll grasp cause-and-effect principles or modify their maladaptive behavior. In fact, lectures, sermons, and punishment can have the opposite effect. Students often become resentful of endless lectures and intentionally disregard repeated admonitions that they don't want to hear.

The antidote for this thoughtlessness is to train LD students to consider what's happening to them and around them and to train them to think more logically. With effective methodical instruction and sufficient practice, these students can acquire the mental reflex of asking:

- "What's going on in this situation?"

- "What are my options?"

- "What are the potential consequences of this decision, attitude, or behavior?"

- "How can I best attain my objective?"

The alternative is to assume that students will naturally develop the capacity to think strategically through some sort of magical osmosis process. This is a risky assumption given the palpable dangers that teenagers face everyday. Adolescents who never learn how to think critically and strategically are at risk for making non-judicious choices throughout their lives. Their flawed choices are likely to have monumental academic, economic, and emotional repercussions.

Activities and Exercises

Considering the Possibilities

Student Book page 193

The introductory anecdote encourages students to evaluate another student's choices and to examine the potential consequences of flawed decisions and wise decisions. The objective is to make the procedure of carefully evaluating the possible and probable effects of choices an automatic response.

Considering the Consequences

Student Book page 196

The answers to decision/consequence match-up are: 1.g 2.n 3.o 4.j 5.m 6.i 7.c 8.q 9.r 10.d 11.l 12.f 13.p 14.b 15.e 16.k 17.a 18.h (Please note: k and j may be switched and still be correct.)

<u>The Decision Point</u>

Student Book page 198

<u>Identifying the Decision Point</u>

Student Book page 199

Your students are constantly faced with choices. Some are inconsequential ("Should I order the apple or cherry pie?"). Others have profoundly important implications ("Should I try this drug?"). Too many students are not aware that they've arrived at a crossroads and do not recognize that they need to make a careful assessment before proceeding. Those who are oblivious to the potential consequences of their choices are far more likely to respond impulsively and thoughtlessly. This exercise underscores the importance of being able to identify critical decision points. The goal is your students to grasp the concept of cause and effect and to recognize the link between choices and potential outcomes.

<u>Describing a Decision Point In Your Own Life</u>

Student Book page 200

Students must be able to link the decision-point phenomenon with actual events in their own life. This exercise is designed to help them make this connection and heighten their awareness that their choices inevitably produce consequences and that these consequences can be positive or negative.

<u>Practice Figuring Out the Effect (or Consequence)</u>

Student Book page 203

<u>Practice Figuring Out the Cause</u>

Student Book page 204

Many students do not realize that the terms *thinking about consequences* and *cause and effect* are often used interchangeably. These exercises introduce the terms "cause" and "effect". The activities heighten awareness of potential consequences and provide repeated opportunities to practice identifying cause-and-effect factors. The exercises also underscore how decision points are usually linked to predictable outcomes. By analyzing common situations, your students will become more aware of how their decisions, behavior, and attitudes influence what occurs in their lives. With sufficient practice, thinking about consequences will become an automatic response.

What Would You Do?

Student Book page 206

Mastery: More Practice Figuring the Cause

Student Book page 207

Identifying the Cause and the Effect

Student Book page 208

Applying Cause and Effect to Your Own Life

Student Book page 208

These exercises help students sharpen their ability to identify cause and effect. The more relevant and applicable they perceive cause-and-effect principles to be, the more likely they are to be guided by these principles when making decisions in their lives.

Answers to **More Practice Figuring Out Causes:** 1.f 2.b 3.j 4.a 5.n 6.d 7.m 8.g 9.k 10.c 11.o 12.h 13.l 14.p 15.e 16.i 17.q

What I Have Learned About Cause and Effect

Student Book page 209

This exercise reinforces cause-and-effect principles and is designed to demonstrate to your students what they have learned about these critically important principles.

Teaching Notes

Unit 15: Heading Off Problems

Objectives:

This unit demonstrates that problems can be avoided when students factor "future time" into their deliberations and decisions and make realistic predictions about what might happen as a consequence of their choices.

Basic Lesson Plan

Student Book pages 211-225

1. Students read **TROUBLE CAN AMBUSH YOU.** They then examine and evaluate Jennifer's options in responding to her friend's flawed decisions and actions (*causes*), and they predict the possible or probable consequences (*effects*).

2. In **MAKING TOUGH DECISIONS**, students explore the issues of making difficult choices and confronting moral and ethical dilemmas. Students complete a moral-dilemma inventory that is designed to encourage introspection. The procedure of carefully and analytically assessing personal decisions should then be examined.

3. Students complete **DOING THE RIGHT THING** and apply a problem/challenge assessment procedure to an actual event in their own lives. They then explore the relevant moral and ethical issues that influenced, or failed to influence, their decision.

4. In **USING YOUR HEAD TO AVOID PROBLEMS,** students respond to hypothetical situations and apply an analytical strategic thinking procedure.

5. Students re-examine the **THINKING-SMART CHECKLIST** introduced in Unit 13. After reassessing four of their original responses, students record their reasons for changes in their attitudes. This exercise encourages further assimilation of the strategic-thinking skills taught in the preceding five units.

6. In **MASTERY: MORE PRACTICE AVOIDING PROBLEMS** and in **WHAT WOULD YOU DO?,** students have additional opportunities to analyze situations and apply problem-avoiding procedures.

Providing an Antidote for Flawed Judgment

No instructional program can help students avoid every problem, miscalculation, and error in judgment. In fact, shielding students from *all* missteps can actually impede their full emotional and intellectual development. Learning how to analyze and handle life's miscues provide vital opportunities for youngsters to hone their thinking skills and acquire insight, judgment, and wisdom. Occasional mistakes and reversals can help students understand and assimilate the all-important principles of cause and effect that influence most of life's endeavors.

A vital distinction must be made between students experiencing sporadic and relatively innocuous setbacks and their becoming enmeshed in a pattern of poor judgment that causes significant setbacks and/or injuries. Such a pattern is frequently psychologically damaging, and the fallout invariably undermines self-esteem.

Virtually, every student occasionally forgets to do a homework assignment, does poorly on a test, talks out of turn, breaks a rule, and suffers a reprimand or punishment. The reactions of the teacher or parent to these misdeeds can be disconcerting, but the mistakes generally have relatively little long-range significance, and most children learn not to repeat these gaffes. Repeated blunders, however, are a red flag that indicates either poor strategic thinking or an unconscious self-sabotaging agenda.

Chronic poor judgment magnifies the already considerable academic challenges that LD students face every day. Students who continually submit incomplete, sloppy, inaccurate, and/or late assignments are not only destined to be on the receiving end of a great deal of negative verbal feedback from their teachers and parents, they are also destined to receive poor grades. If this dynamic is to change, these students must be guided to the realization that they are responsible for the predictable consequences of their attitudes, behavior, and decisions.

Unless chronically flawed decision-making is addressed, the self-defeating behavior could become an ingrained component in an LD student's personality and *modus operandi.* *

---

* **ADD/ADHD can be a primary source of chronic and seemingly willful self-sabotaging behavior.**

The long-range implications can be disastrous. In addition to marginal academic performance, students who act mindlessly and disregard the implications of their behavior are more likely to experience accidents and injury, have fragile self-esteem, experiment with drugs, steal, join gangs, engage in violence, and act promiscuously.

The over-riding objective is to help LD students recognize their pivotal role in and responsibility for the negative events occurring in their lives. Although this awareness can be instrumental in redirecting counterproductive behavior, awareness alone may not resolve the problem of chronic poor judgment, especially in the case of students with poor self-esteem who have an unconscious "self-destruct" agenda and appear intent on undermining themselves. Self-sabotaging behavior driven by deep-seated emotional conflicts requires professional intervention in the form of counseling or psychotherapy.

Activities and Exercises

Trouble Can Ambush You

Student Book page 211

After reading the anecdote, students analyze Jennifer's dilemma as she struggles to help her friend Ashley avoid making a serious mistake. Students identify and evaluate Jennifer's decisions and consider her options in responding to the challenge she faces. The intent of the exercise is for students to develop a heightened awareness of the process of carefully weighing the pros and cons and to make this awareness an integral component in their evaluative process. The activity segues into the critically important issues of recognizing and handling moral and ethical dilemmas and factoring personal values into the decision-making procedure. The goal is for students to become more conscious of their values and for them to make decisions that are congruent with what is moral and ethical.

Making Tough Decisions

Student Book page 216

In this exercise, students are asked to wrestle with the moral and ethical issues that are raised in the introductory anecdote and to complete a **Moral/Ethical Dilemma Inventory**. You, of course, want to avoid telling students how to evaluate the issues, as this would defeat the intent of the activity, which is to help students develop their *own* critical thinking skills and their *own* moral and ethical compass.

Students should be encouraged to draw their own conclusions about the issues and to express their feelings about how they themselves would handle similar situations. Ask probing questions that elicit analytical thinking and reasoned judgment, but do so with care. Students may not perceive the issues from your personal moral or ethical perspective. Your role is to serve as a guide and help students achieve insight and acquire wisdom. Sermons, lectures, and a litany of "do's and don'ts" are likely only to trigger resistance and resentment.

This exercise encourages self-examination and introspection. For some students, and especially those who have a history of acting impulsively and mindlessly, being introspective is likely to be an alien experience. These youngsters may resist examining their behavior, feelings, and values, and some may even be quite threatened by the process. You want students to acquire the habit of considering *in advance* how they might respond in situations that involve honesty, ethics, legality, and loyalty to friends. This future-oriented thinking can dramatically reduce the risk of their making seriously flawed choices that could alter the course of their lives.

Doing the Right Thing

Student Book page 217

This exercise is designed to make the analytical thinking and introspection relevant. Students examine a real event in their lives and apply cause-and-effect principles in analyzing this event. They are asked to consider potential consequences and ethical issue they may not have considered when the event actually occurred.

Using Your Head to Avoid Problems

Student Book page 218

All students will encounter situations that could result in physical or emotional injury. Those who carefully examine their options at critical decision-making crossroads can considerably reduce the risks.

You want your students to develop the automatic habit of asking themselves key questions before they act. These might include:

- "Should I take a chance and swim in this river?"

- "Should I tell my mom the truth?"
- "Should I agree to participate in this?"
- "Should I jump from this bridge into the stream?"
- "Should I go surfing with this undertow?"

The goal is for students to think ahead and factor the potential impact of their behavior into their decisions and behavior. Students who do not acquire these capabilities are likely to have recurring disastrous collisions in life that could irreparably damage them.

Re-Examining the Thinking-Smart Checklist

Student Book page 220

Your students have now almost completed the program, and it would be beneficial for them to re-examine and reconsider their initial responses to the **Thinking-Smart Checklist** introduced on pages 191-192. Asking them to reconsider the rationale for their original reaction is intended to reinforce mastery of the concepts that have been introduced.

Encourage students to change their original responses if they so desire. If they now are capable of analyzing the described situations more strategically, any changes they make testify to the progress they have made in applying strategic-thinking principles. When discussing the checklist, be prepared for some responses still to be off-target. You obviously want to react with sensitivity and avoid unintentionally making students feel uncomfortable.

The acquisition of critical- and strategic-thinking skills is an incremental process. Some children "get it" more quickly than others. Others struggle and have greater difficulty applying reason, logic, and judgment. Patience is vital. If certain students still have off-target responses, you may want them to repeat components of the program that address their specific deficiencies.

Mastery: More Practice Avoiding Problems

Student Book page 221

This exercise provides an additional opportunity for your students to apply the problem-avoiding process to a real-life situation. The activity encourages them to use forethought *before* a crisis develops.

What Would You Do?

Student Book page 223

In this exercise, your students apply the strategic-thinking, problem-avoiding procedure to a series of hypothetical situations. This final exercise is intended to reinforce mastery of the process.

Teaching Notes

Unit 16: Power-Thinking

Objectives:

This unit reviews the range of components that comprise the nuts and bolts of strategic thinking, problem-solving, and effective studying. It also encourages the consistent application of the skills that have been taught in the program.

Basic Lesson Plan

Student Book pages 227-238

1. Students read **GENERATING MAXIMUM BRAIN POWER.** They complete a self-assessment and evaluate their scores.

2. Students review and are given additional opportunities to practice using **DIBS** when confronted with problems.

3. Students are guided to the realization that strategic thinking is the underlying principle in *common sense* and *using your head.* The procedures of anticipating consequences, analyzing situations before acting, and learning from mistakes in judgment are practiced and reinforced.

4. Students practice using **DIBS** to deal with temptations.

5. Students evaluate a range of behaviors and attitudes and categorize the behaviors and attitudes as examples of "using your head" and "not using your head."

Acquiring Perspective

Despite evidence of improvement, your students may not fully appreciate the progress that they have made. By encouraging them to step back and inventory what they have learned, you can play an instrumental role in reinforcing their self-awareness, self-confidence, and self-appreciation.

Students who complete this program now possess an array of powerful thinking and academic tools. These tools, however, are of little value if students are not committed to using them. This unit is intended to tie the ends together and underscore the need for consistent application of what has been learned.

In this final unit, students review the problem-solving, goal-setting, and analytical-thinking components of the program. They complete an inventory that prompts them to consider whether they are utilizing the new techniques that they have learned. They also are provided with several additional opportunities to apply the **DIBS** method, and they examine the importance of making conscious decisions to use good judgment whenever they are faced with circumstances that could potentially affect their academic, physical, or emotional well-being. Students examine other important issues that include learning from and not repeating mistakes; saying *"no"* when confronted with situations that could produce harmful effects, and handling temptations that could be counterproductive or dangerous.

Establishing the Habit of Success and Achievement

The **Winning the Study Game Program** your students are about to complete is based on five key premises:

1. **Students who possess effective study habits are far more likely to succeed academically than those who lack these skills.**
2. **Success is habit-forming.**
3. **Academic achievement generates self-confidence, pride, motivation, and the desire for more success.**
4. **Strategic thinking is a powerful life-enhancing resource that can be methodically taught and easily learned.**
5. **Students who think strategically manifest specific achievement-oriented attitudes and behaviors. They are goal-directed, plan ahead, consider potential consequences, prevail over challenges, analyze and solve problems, assess and learn from mistakes, and bounce back from setbacks.**

The thrill of achievement and pride in one's accomplishments are addictive. Students who are convinced that they can succeed academically, handle challenges, attain their goals, and deal with life's setbacks are immediately distinguishable. They are motivated and diligent, and they radiate self-assurance.

Activities and Exercises

Assessing What You Have Learned about Study Skills

Student Book pages 229

This exercise asks students to examine a range of skills that have been previously taught. The activity is designed to encourage self-assessment and to motivate students to improve their performance in areas where they may still be deficient.

If students have not mastered certain specific skills, it would be advisable to have them review the particular units in which these skills were introduced. An effective way to broach this review is to use your students' self-assessment on the Thinking-Smart Checklist on pages 191-192. You might say: "You indicated on the checklist that you're still having difficulty making a study plan, budgeting time, and taking notes from lectures. Let's quickly review the units that deal with these issues. I'm certain that after a quick review, you'll feel much more comfortable using these skills."

Reviewing the DIBS Problem-Solving Method

Student Book page 230

Final Practice with DIBS

Student Book pages 231

The goal of this exercise is to review the **DIBS** problem-solving method by demonstrating how the method could be used to deal with test anxiety. The exercise also provides students with another opportunity to apply **DIBS** to a real-world problem.

Common Sense and Using Your Head

Student Book page 232

This exercise links strategic thinking with the terms "common sense" and "using your head." The exercise underscores two key strategic-thinking principles:

- Students can avoid making mistakes and judgment errors when they get into the habit of thinking about what they are doing and the potential consequences of their actions and attitudes.

- Students can avoid repeating mistakes if they establish the habit of carefully analyzing and learning from their setbacks.

Handling Temptations

Student Book page 234

Students are continually faced with temptations. These might include such things as: "Should I put off reading a book for my book report until next week?," "Should I disregard what my dad told me and go to the party anyway?," "Should I try this pill this kid is offering me?," "Should I cheat on the science test?," "Should I plagiarize from the encyclopedia?," "Should I join a gang?," or "Should I attempt to load my dad's gun?"

This exercise underscores again how students can use **DIBS** to assess situations rationally and resist temptations that could wreak havoc with their lives. This capacity will be an important resource throughout life.

Deciding What's Smart

Student Book page 236

In this activity, students are asked to classify a range of attitudes, decisions, and behaviors. This provides them with an opportunity to review previously taught skills and practice analytical thinking.

Feeling Proud, Powerful, and Self-Confident

Student Book page 238

Of the many stated objectives of the **Winning the Study Game Program**, the enhancement of your students' self-appreciation and self-confidence ranks among the most important. Although your students' ultimate choice of careers can obviously affect their income and social status, their decision to become a teacher, surgeon, scientist, mechanic, attorney, professional athlete, or electrician is beyond your control. What matters is that students learn to respect and value themselves, their talents, and their intrinsic worth as a human being. Good skills, a successful track record in school, pride in a job well-done, and recognition of one's competencies produce *healthy egoism.* This positive "sense of self" is distinct from the self-aggrandizement and narcissism associated with *egotism.*

Children express healthy egoism when they assert their faith in their ability to cause positive things to happen in their lives. Egoism is the fuel that motivates them to establish personal goals, to test themselves and their talents, to develop their abilities, and to achieve. Without egoism, towering skyscrapers would never be built, symphonies would never be written, and disease-fighting vaccines would never be discovered.

As a special education professional, you have many functions and responsibilities. One of the most critical of these obligations is to encourage LD students to extend the boundaries of their expectations and aspirations and to stretch for rewards beyond their immediate grasp. When they finally snag the brass ring, they will glow with pride. This pride is far more significant than their being able to remember how many miles separate the earth and the moon or being able to name of the fourth President of the United States.

Throughout this program, a metaphor has been used thematically. This metaphor compares a student's engaged, thinking brain to a powerful engine. Your job has been to show your students how to engage this engine. You'll know that you have attained your objective when you see your students sitting confidently and alertly in the driver's seat, pointed toward their destination, and responsibly in control of the power that they command.

Appendix

107

My Weekly Schedule

TIME	Monday	Tuesday	Wednesday	Thursday	Friday
3:15 - 3:30					
3:30 - 4:00					
4:00 - 4:30					
4:30 - 5:00					
5:00 - 5:30					
5:30 - 6:00					
6:00 – 6:30					
6:30 - 7:00					
7:00 - 7:30					
7:30 - 8:00					
8:00 - 8:30					
8:30 - 9:00					
9:00 - 9:30					
9:30 -10:00					

Code: [ ] free time [ ] studying [ ] dinner [ ] sleep [ ] _____ *

[ ] _____   [ ] _____   [ ] _____

*religious school, music practice, Scouts, after-school athletics, tutoring, chores, etc.

My Study-Schedule Contract

To Whom It May Concern:

I, _____ (your name), agree to use my study schedule every day for a **2-week trial period.** If I decide after two weeks that the schedule needs to be adjusted, I can make changes. Once I make these changes, I agree to use the new schedule for a minimum of **4 additional weeks**. If I am pleased with the results and my school-work improves, I will continue to use the schedule for the rest of the school year. I can make changes in the schedule every four weeks. Once I make these adjustments, I will use the schedule for another 4 weeks before making changes.

Finally, I agree to keep to my schedule without having to be reminded by my parents.

Your Signature:

_____

Your Teacher's Signature:

_____

Date:

_____

Your Parent's Signature:

_____

Practice Assignment Sheet

SUBJECTS	MONDAY	TUESDAY	WEDNESDAY	THURSDAY	FRIDAY
Math					
Social Studies					
English					
Science					
Tests & Reports					

My Personal Assignment Sheet

SUBJECTS	MONDAY	TUESDAY	WEDNESDAY	THURSDAY	FRIDAY
_____					
_____					
_____					
_____					
Tests & Reports					

Checklist #1 -- Materials to Bring Home

	Mon.	Tues.	Wed.	Thurs.	Fri.
Binder	_____	_____	_____	_____	_____
Textbooks	_____	_____	_____	_____	_____
Assignment Sheet	_____	_____	_____	_____	_____
Workbooks	_____	_____	_____	_____	_____
Handouts	_____	_____	_____	_____	_____
Study Guides	_____	_____	_____	_____	_____
Corrected Assignments	_____	_____	_____	_____	_____
Graded Tests	_____	_____	_____	_____	_____
_____	_____	_____	_____	_____	_____
_____	_____	_____	_____	_____	_____
_____	_____	_____	_____	_____	_____
_____	_____	_____	_____	_____	_____

Checklist #2 -- Materials to Bring to School

	Mon.	Tues.	Wed.	Thurs.	Fri.
Binder	_____	_____	_____	_____	_____
Textbooks	_____	_____	_____	_____	_____
Assignment Sheet	_____	_____	_____	_____	_____
Workbooks	_____	_____	_____	_____	_____
Study Guides	_____	_____	_____	_____	_____
Completed Homework	_____	_____	_____	_____	_____
Paper	_____	_____	_____	_____	_____
Pencils and Pens	_____	_____	_____	_____	_____
_____	_____	_____	_____	_____	_____
_____	_____	_____	_____	_____	_____
_____	_____	_____	_____	_____	_____

Checklist #3 -- Home Study Environment

	Mon.	Tues.	Wed.	Thurs.	Fri.
Quiet Study Area	_____	_____	_____	_____	_____
Desk or Table	_____	_____	_____	_____	_____
Dictionary	_____	_____	_____	_____	_____
Paper	_____	_____	_____	_____	_____
Pencils and Pens	_____	_____	_____	_____	_____
Ruler	_____	_____	_____	_____	_____
Books and Study Materials	_____	_____	_____	_____	_____
_____	_____	_____	_____	_____	_____
_____	_____	_____	_____	_____	_____
_____	_____	_____	_____	_____	_____

Keeping Track of My Performance During the Experiment

Subject: _____

Homework:

Date:_____ Grade:_____   Date:_____ Grade:_____

Date:_____ Grade:_____   Date:_____ Grade:_____

Date:_____ Grade:_____   Date:_____ Grade:_____

Date:_____ Grade:_____   Date:_____ Grade:_____

Date:_____ Grade:_____   Date:_____ Grade:_____

Tests:

Date:_____ Grade:_____   Date:_____ Grade:_____

Date:_____ Grade:_____   Date:_____ Grade:_____

Date:_____ Grade:_____   Date:_____ Grade:_____

Subject: _____

Homework:

Date:_____ Grade:_____   Date:_____ Grade:_____

Date:_____ Grade:_____   Date:_____ Grade:_____

Date:_____ Grade:_____   Date:_____ Grade:_____

Date:_____ Grade:_____   Date:_____ Grade:_____

Date:_____ Grade:_____   Date:_____ Grade:_____

Tests:

Date:_____ Grade:_____   Date:_____ Grade:_____

Date:_____ Grade:_____   Date:_____ Grade:_____

Date:_____ Grade:_____   Date:_____ Grade:_____

My Personal Performance Chart
Test Results

GRADES

A
B
C
D
F

DATE

My Personal Performance Chart
Homework Results

GRADES

A
B
C
D
F

DATE

Keeping Track of My Performance

Day:_____   **Date**_____

Subject:	Test Grades:	Reports:	Homework:	In-class Work:
_____	_____	_____	_____	_____
_____	_____	_____	_____	_____
_____	_____	_____	_____	_____
_____	_____	_____	_____	_____
_____	_____	_____	_____	_____

Keeping Track of My Performance

Day:_____   **Date**_____

Subject:	Test Grades:	Reports:	Homework:	In-class Work:
_____	_____	_____	_____	_____
_____	_____	_____	_____	_____
_____	_____	_____	_____	_____
_____	_____	_____	_____	_____
_____	_____	_____	_____	_____

Sample Mind-Map

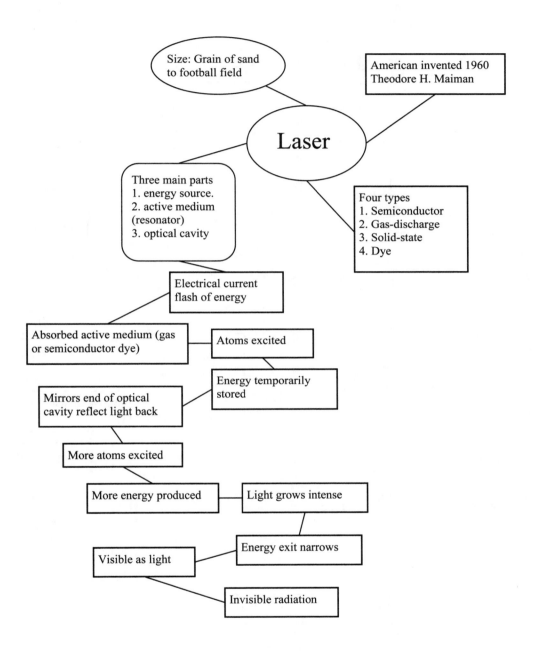

Completed Mind-Map

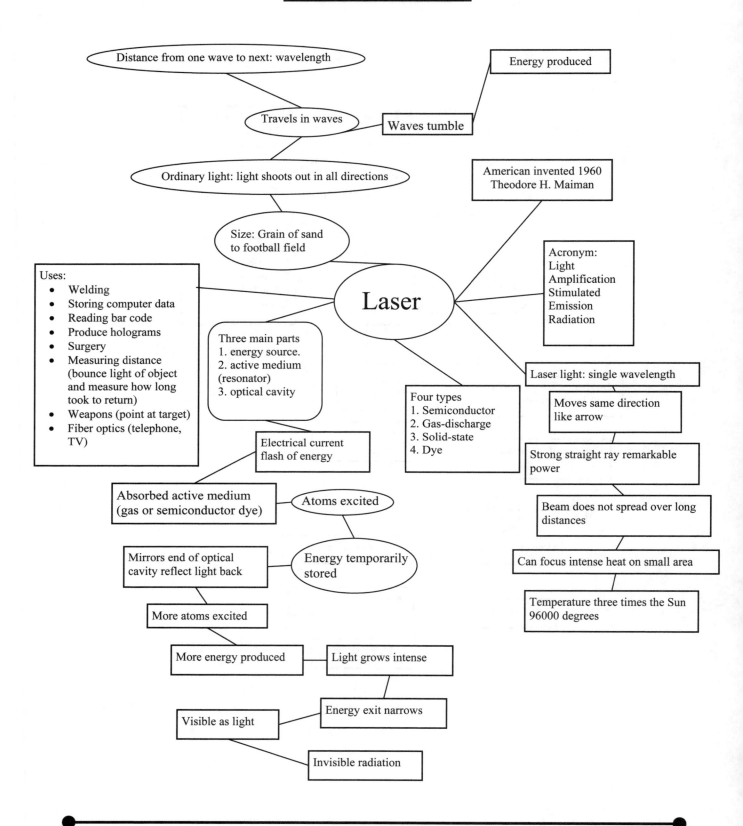

LASERS

Expanding the Frontiers of Science and Technology

Imagine a very narrow beam of light capable of drilling two hundred holes on a spot as tiny as the head of a pin and powerful enough to pierce a diamond, the hardest natural substance. This intense beam of light can be also be used to trigger a small nuclear reaction or to reach the moon more than 250,000 miles away.

In 1960, an American scientist named Theodore H. Maiman built a machine that could produce this light. He called his invention a laser. The word is an *acronym* whose letters stand for Light Amplification by Stimulated Emission of Radiation.

Types of Lasers

Today there are four main types of lasers: solid-state, semiconductor, gas-discharge, and dye lasers. These devices can range in size from as small as a grain of salt to as large as a football field.

Transforming Energy into Intense Light

Lasers typically have three main parts: an *energy source*, a substance called an *active medium* (also called a *resonator*), and a structure enclosing the active medium known as an *optical cavity*. The energy source typically supplies an electric current. The flash of energy is absorbed by the active medium. The atoms in the active medium--usually a gas or synthetic material--are excited, and the energy level increases. This energy is temporarily stored and then discharged in the form of light waves. Mirrors at the ends of the optical cavity reflect the light back into the active medium. More atoms are excited, and additional energy is produced. The light grows increasingly intense. The energy exits the laser as a narrow beam that may be visible, or invisible when the beam is comprised exclusively of radiation.

Distinguishing Ordinary Light from Laser Light

The light discharged by the excited particles in a laser differs from the light produced by a light bulb or fluorescent lamp. In the case of a florescent lamp, a current of electricity excites the electrons in the mercury vapor inside the tube. The waves of light shoot out in all directions and do not reach very far. This explains why there may be dark shadows in the corners of a large room even though the lights are turned on.

Ordinary light travels like ocean waves during a storm. The distance from the top of one wave to the next is called a *wavelength*. Because the different wavelengths tumble over each other and travel in many directions at once, the total amount of produced energy is low.

Unlike ordinary light, the beam produced by a laser consists of a single wavelength. The waves move in the same direction like an arrow. The result is a strong, straight ray that has remarkable power.

A laser beam does not spread out over long distances. A beam aimed at the moon might light up a spot only two or three miles wide. Although an ordinary beam of light from a searchlight could not possibly reach the moon, if it could, the lighted area would spread out more than 25,000 miles!

Because a laser beam is a *single* wavelength, it can focus intense light and heat on a very small area. A laser beam can actually generate heat three times as hot as the temperature of the sun which is 32,000 degrees Fahrenheit!

Using Lasers

Lasers can be found in homes, factories, stores, offices, hospitals, and libraries. The intense light has many applications that include welding tiny, intricate electronic circuits, storing computer data, and reading the prices recorded on the bar code for items in a store. Lasers can also be used to record music, make movies, and produce three-dimensional images called holograms. These holograms are imprinted on credit cards and on advertising displays, artwork, and jewelry.

Surgeons use lasers to perform delicate operations such as welding a detached retina back to the eyeball. A laser can also be used as a scalpel to remove tumors, scars, or even tattoos. Because the intense heat stops the flow of blood, there is very little bleeding during surgery.

Lasers are also useful in measuring distances. By pointing the beam at a target, technicians can measure the exact time required for the beam to bounce back. In contrast, radar bounces an electronic pulse off an object and measures how long it takes for the pulse to bounce back. Because light-beam measurement can indicate the target's location and distance with great accuracy, scientists regularly use lasers to track satellites that are specially equipped with light-reflecting mirrors.

The straight-line beam of the laser also has many military applications. A weapon with a laser sight can aim a beam of light on a target. Because the beam shows precisely where the bullet, missile, or bomb will hit, weapons equipped with lasers are highly accurate and reliable.

Fiber-optics communication is another field where lasers have great value. The electrical signals of telephone calls and televisions pictures are transformed into pulses or bursts of laser light. Thin strands of glass called optical fibers conduct the light. These strands are no thicker than a human hair. All the energy is passed through the fiber, and one fiber can carry as much information as several thousand copper telephone wires. A single beam could actually transmit all the information in an encyclopedia in a fraction of a second!

Today, lasers are essential tools in virtually every area. In the years ahead, new and even more remarkable uses will undoubtedly be discovered. These applications will continually expand the frontiers of science and technology.

CLEOPATRA

One of the Most Fascinating Queens in History

More than two thousand years ago, an extraordinary young woman named Cleopatra ascended the throne in Egypt. Although portrayed in books and movies as being exceptionally beautiful, Cleopatra was actually quite plain. Her most striking qualities were her wit, charm, and intelligence. An historian of the period reported that Cleopatra could speak eight languages and described her as one of the most brilliant women of her time.

The Struggle for Power in Egypt

Cleopatra was the last in a dynasty (rulers of the same family) founded by a general named Ptolemy in 323 B.C. She became queen of Egypt in 51 B.C. when her father Ptolemy XII died. Only seventeen at the time, she was forced to share her power with her ten-year-old brother, Ptolemy XIII, who also became her husband. Such a marriage would be illegal today, but in Egyptian royal families during this era, marriage between a brother and sister was common.

The guardians of Ptolemy XIII wanted him to rule Egypt alone, and they plotted against Cleopatra. Successful in seizing power, they drove Cleopatra from the throne and forced her into exile.

In 48 B.C., a famous Roman general named Caesar invaded Egypt with his army and arrived in Alexandria, Egypt's capital. Caesar was pursuing a rival general named Pompey with whom he was struggling for power in Rome.

Realizing that Caesar could help her defeat Ptolemy and that he could help her regain the throne, Cleopatra decided to win Caesar's support. Because she was afraid he would not agree to see her, she supposedly hid herself in a carpet and had one of her servants carry the carpet to Caesar. Very impressed with Cleopatra's cleverness, Caesar agreed to help her. In 47 B.C. his army defeated Ptolemy's forces in battle. Ptolemy drowned while attempting to escape.

Caesar put Cleopatra back on the throne and fell in love with the young queen. In 46 B.C., Caesar invited Cleopatra to visit Rome. She accepted. Certain politicians in Rome feared that Caesar wanted to make himself king. To prevent this, they assassinated him in 44 B.C. on the steps of the Roman Senate.

Some historians believe that Cleopatra wanted to become Caesar's queen after he became king of the Roman Empire. She may have dreamed about joining the two kingdoms, but no one can be certain. If she did have a secret agenda, the plans disintegrated when Caesar was assassinated. Cleopatra realized that unless she returned to Egypt, she too might be killed.

Mark Antony

Mark Antony led an army against those responsible for the assassination of Caesar and defeated them. After the battle, three men shared power in Rome: Mark Antony, Lepidus, and Octavian, Caesar's nephew. These men became the rulers of the Roman Empire. Soon after Caesar's death, Mark Antony went to Asia Minor with his army.

Mark Antony had met Cleopatra during her stay in Rome. He wrote Cleopatra and asked her to visit him in Asia Minor. Wanting to rule Rome alone, he was hoping to obtain money from Cleopatra and to form an alliance against Caesar's nephew, Octavian.

Although she was unsure of his motives, the twenty-nine-year-old queen sailed from Alexandria to meet Mark Antony. Upon her arrival, she invited him to visit her aboard her magnificent royal barge. As Caesar had been before him, Mark Antony was captivated by Cleopatra's charm and wit. They fell in love. They were later married, and Cleopatra gave birth to twins, a boy and a girl.

The Civil War in Rome

While Mark Antony was in Asia Minor with Cleopatra, Octavian ruled Rome. Octavian believed that Mark Antony was the lovestruck victim of a wicked, greedy and ambitious temptress and that he had had become her puppet. In 32 B.C., a civil war broke out for control of the Roman Empire. Octavian and Mark Antony were now bitter enemies.

Antony was an excellent general, but his army had been badly weakened during the conquest of Parthia. Historians have also suggested that Antony was spoiled by luxury and was no longer as talented as he had been during previous battles. In 31 B.C., the fleets of Mark Antony and Cleopatra were defeated when they were attacked off the coast of western Greece by Octavian's ships at the Battle of Actium.

The Return to Alexandria

Antony and Cleopatra fled with their remaining ships to Alexandria. Octavian pursued them and laid siege to the city. During this siege, thousands of Antony's soldiers deserted.

Cleopatra spread a false report that she had committed suicide. Antony learned of her supposed death. In despair, he attempted to kill himself by falling on his sword. Before he died, he found out that Cleopatra was actually still alive. He asked his followers to carry him to her. Barely alive, Antony begged Cleopatra to save herself. Soon after, he died in her arms.

When Cleopatra met with Octavian after Mark Antony's death, she tried to make peace with him, but she failed. Fearing Octavian would publicly humiliate and then murder her, she decided to commit suicide.

Cleopatra asked Octavian for permission to visit Mark Antony's tomb. In a basket of figs, she had hidden a small deadly snake called an asp. Taking the snake from the basket, she let it sink its fangs into her neck. When Octavian's soldiers returned, they found her dead by Antony's side. Cleopatra was thirty-nine years old.

The historian Plutarch reported that Octavian ordered a magnificent funeral for the two lovers. He also commanded that their bodies be placed side by side for people to see.

Many believe that Cleopatra failed because she was too ambitious. Certainly she captivated two of the greatest Romans of her era, Caesar and Mark Antony. She failed, however, to captivate another powerful Roman, and this man destroyed her. His name was Octavian.

A Letter to Myself -- My Goals in School

Date: _____

My Name: _____

My Address: _____

_____

Dear Me:

I'm writing this letter to myself to record my current **long-term goals** and **short-term academic goals**. I understand that I can change my goals later, but I agree not to change my long-term and short-term goals for the next three months. I will tape this letter near my desk or on the wall near my bed. I will periodically review my short-term goals to remind myself of my objectives and to make certain that I am doing all that I can to attain the grades I have targeted.

LONG-TERM GOALS

1._____

2._____

3._____

4._____

SPECIFIC SHORT-TERM ACADEMIC GOALS

<u>Subject</u>	<u>Most Recent Report-Card Grades</u>	<u>Grade I Want on Next Report Card</u>
Math	_____	_____
_____	_____	_____
_____	_____	_____
_____	_____	_____
_____	_____	_____
_____	_____	_____

Yours truly,

_____

Weekly Goal Sheet

Week #___   YES   NO

Weekly Goal: _____

Daily Goals:

Mon.:   _____   ____   ____

Tues.:   _____   ____   ____

Wed.:   _____   ____   ____

Thurs.:   _____   ____   ____

Fri.:   _____   ____   ____

Week #___   YES   NO

Weekly Goal: _____

Daily Goals:

Mon.:   _____   ____   ____

Tues.:   _____   ____   ____

Wed.:   _____   ____   ____

Thurs.:   _____   ____   ____

Fri.:   _____   ____   ____

Week #___   YES   NO

Weekly Goal: _____

Daily Goals:

Mon.:   _____   ____   ____

Tues.:   _____   ____   ____

Wed.:   _____   ____   ____

Thurs.:   _____   ____   ____

Fri.:   _____   ____   ____

My Strategy

My Long-Term Goal: _____

Steps to get the job done successfully and achieve the goal: (These are your short-term goals.)

My grades:

1._____

2._____

3._____

Impressing my teachers:

1._____

2._____

Planning my education (courses)

1._____

2._____

3._____

Job training

1._____

2._____

What problems might I face?

1._____

2._____

3._____

Whom could I ask for help?

1._____

2._____

Notes

_____

_____

_____

_____

_____

_____

_____

_____

_____

_____

_____

_____

_____

_____

_____

_____

_____

_____

_____

_____

_____

_____

Notes:

_____

_____

_____

_____

_____

_____

_____

_____

_____

_____

_____

_____

_____

_____

_____

_____

_____

_____

_____

_____

_____

_____

_____

Notes:

_____

_____

_____

_____

_____

_____

_____

_____

_____

_____

_____

_____

_____

_____

_____

_____

_____

_____

_____

_____

_____

Notes:

_____

_____

_____

_____

_____

_____

_____

_____

_____

_____

_____

_____

_____

_____

_____

_____

_____

_____

_____

_____

The **Winning the Study Game Program**
titles are currently available in the following formats.

Winning the Study Game – Guide for Resource Specialists
1-890455-46-6
Perfect bound / lay flat binding / Catalog # P800

Winning the Study Game – Learning How to Succeed in School
Consumable Student Edition 1-890455-47-4
Perfect bound / lay flat binding / three-hole punched / Catalog #P801

Winning the Study Game – Learning How to Succeed in School
Reproducible Student Edition 1-890455-48-2
Perfect bound / lay flat binding / Catalog #P802

Winning the Study Game – Learning How to Succeed in School
Reproducible Student Edition **CD ROM** / Catalog #P803

If you have questions, would like to request a catalog, or to place an order,
please contact *Peytral Publications, Inc.*
We will be happy to help you.

Peytral Publications, Inc.
PO Box 1162
Minnetonka, MN   55345-0162

Toll free order line: (877) 739-8725
Questions: (952) 949-8707
Fax: (952) 906-9777

Or visit us online at:
www.peytral.com